MARX & ENGELS

MARX & ENGELS

The Intellectual Relationship

Terrell Carver

Lecturer in Politics,
University of Bristol

INDIANA UNIVERSITY PRESS
BLOOMINGTON

Manufactured in Great Britain

Library of Congress catalog card number: 83-48679
ISBN: 0-253-33681-3

For
MRG

Contents

Preface

By its very nature the story of a relationship is complex, and that of an intellectual relationship particularly so, since a double, interactive, and (when one partner survives) even retrospective development must be analysed. I hope that the reader will find the Marx–Engels chronology at the end of the book useful in following my account of two complicated careers and of a famous relationship that has very nearly taken on a life of its own.

I am grateful to the University of Bristol, its Library, and the Department of Politics for supporting me in this project.

Bristol
December 1982

Terrell Carver

Introduction

In this book I aim to take a factual look at the Marx–Engels intellectual relationship in order to answer a specific set of questions: Why was the first meeting between Marx and Engels unsuccessful? What then attracted Marx to Engels in 1844 when the partnership was founded? What effect did Engels's work have on Marx? What exactly was clarified in the jointly written *German Ideology* and for whom? When did the 'dialectics', made famous by Engels, first emerge? What was the relationship between Marx and Engels in their mature years? To what extent is the account of the relationship given by Engels after Marx's death an accurate one? What bearing does the Marx–Engels intellectual relationship have on our reading of their respective works?

In answering these questions I have striven to avoid certain fallacies which are all too common in the literature on Marx, Engels and Marxism. The first is the 'mirror' fallacy: if the commentator does not understand a work by Marx or a passage in one of his works, *Marx* must have been confused, i.e. as confused as the commentator. Too many commentators opt much too quickly for an ascription of confusion in order, fallaciously, to 'solve' a problem in textual interpretation. In my view much more sense can be made of Marx's work than is commonly supposed. Curiously, commentators are much less reluctant to ascribe confusion to Engels, whose works, the reader will discover, suffer from very considerable ambiguities of which he was apparently unaware.

The second fallacy is the 'chronological' one, and its converse: when an idea first appears in, for example, Marx's surviving works, then that is the first time that he had that idea; and conversely, whenever Marx first had an idea, he immediately wrote it down. It surprises me very much how scrupulous concern with textual dating goes for nought when such dates are used to 'prove' that the intellectual context of successive works is radically different, when more plausible psychological assumptions, and a more thorough attention to the intended audience and other circumstances surrounding the production of a text, might lead to a theory of intellectual development that is admittedly more complex, but arguably more accurate and much more informative. The chronological care lavished on Marx's texts has little parallel in commentary on Engels, whose writings, so I shall argue, changed in a more dramatic manner than Marx's over the years, and whose comments on some subjects need crucially to be related to one date in particular, that of Marx's death.

The third fallacy concerns a teleological conception of intellectual dvelopment itself: in many accounts Marx's career is conceived as a series of logically related stages, e.g. romanticism, liberalism, Hegelianism, and Feuerbachianism, which lead as a succession to an 'end', namely the 'self-clarification' which Marx mentions as a feature of *The German Ideology*. In these accounts Marx is presented as somehow imprisoned intellectually within each stage as a kind of 'cell', yet magically granted the right key in producing each 'key' text, in order to unlock that particular 'cell' and proceed to the next.

While there is considerable continuity of a developmental sort in Marx's early (and indeed later) works, a mysterious teleology is not required in explanation. Marx's political interests and circumstances provide a sufficient clue, the one he himself offered in his own autobiographical sketch. Moreover the imprisoning stages are wholly untrue to the powerful yet voraciously sceptical intellect displayed in his works. While he made use of others' views, that fact alone hardly makes him a Hegelian, Feuerbachian, or whatever, and he signally fails stronger tests of discipleship. His intensely ruminative, investigative and scientific approach, in that he demanded evidence for statements and did not in general spin out propositions according to his fancy, itself solves the apparent mystery of his development. His method served his political interest in tackling issues, writers and circumstances that figured in his milieu; the issues, writers and circumstances did not determine stages in what is often, and erroneously, presented as a wholly intellectual metamorphosis.

Curiously a much better case for issues, writers and circumstances setting intellectual limits round a thinker during given periods can be made out with respect to Engels, since his early development lacked Marx's single-minded political thrust and unifying sense of vocation. Engels seemed at times to generate published opinions on whatever subjects were put to him, and he passes some fairly strong tests of discipleship, e.g. to Young Germany, Young Hegelianism, communism of the 1840s and the Marxism of later years. Since there has been so little consideration of his career, however, no one has fastened on a *telos* which he fulfilled in his latter days. While my conception of his career is not teleological, I do have a view on where exactly he found his vocation and what significance this had for his own thought, and for interpretations of Marx.

For reasons that will become clear, the role of Engels, personally and intellectually, is absolutely crucial for a satisfactory understanding of the Marx–Engels intellectual relationship. That is why a great deal of this book is concerned with an analysis of Engels's work in the first instance, and Marx's in the second. This reverses the usual procedure in considering the two and their relationship, when their relationship is considered explicitly or even raised at all. The relationship is a great deal more important than most commentators seem to think, and only by focussing on Engels's life and works can the facts be properly sorted out.

Broadly speaking, commentators on Marx and Marxism take one of three views on the Marx–Engels relationship, none of which is supported by this book. The first view is that Marx and Engels were perfect partners in agreement on all points. Moreover they were the authors of supplementary and/or interchangeable works reflecting a coincidence of interests in some and a division of labour with respect to others. An examination of texts refutes this story, particularly in carefully comparing works by Engels, written after 1859, with Marx's *œuvre*, and in thoroughly examining both sides of any relevant exchange in their correspondence. Most academic commentators now consider this account of the Marx–Engels relation-ship to be untenable. It lingers for political reasons, and in some cases because idle writers find it an easy option.

The second view is that in considering Marx, Engels may be safely ignored. It is significant that no one has tried the reverse procedure, and that fact is a clue to the defects inherent in declining to consider Engels's numerous commentaries on Marx's work, since material from those commentaries may then creep into an interpretation of Marx unknown to the commentator. Engels's version of Marx's work has had very wide currency, and that fact must be acknowledged.

The third view is the most interesting and the most prevalent in scholarly circles: the later Marx, from 1859 onwards, is said to have adopted the 'determinist' views espoused by Engels in the same period, or less strongly, to have agreed with them, drifted towards them, or tolerated them tacitly. The most astonishing thing about this view is that practically no evidence is ever cited to support it; it is simply asserted as true, though never as if it were self-evidently so (which it is not). It is then particularly difficult to engage, since the burden of proof lies with the sceptic, who must additionally supply plausible material (thus compromising his or her own case) in order to produce a refutation.

This 'determinist' view entails a number of substantial theses about Marx, though commentators do not always state them explicitly: 1) that his later, 'determinist' works are inconsistent with his earlier 'philosophical' and/or 'humanist' ones; 2) that the later Marx espoused this 'determinism' inconsistently, because an examination of his later works reveals substantial continuities (in form of words and content) with the earlier material. This double schizophrenia in Marx is never satis-factorily confronted, but is often served up to the reader, who is not encouraged to question its plausibility, psychological or otherwise. Moreover the fact that the view is merely put, rather than argued for, generates vagueness concerning what aspects of the works by the later Marx and Engels are actually at stake. It is not clear wherein this determinism manifests itself exactly, and what is and is not an instance of it. Because of this vagueness the prospect of sorting out similarities and dif-ferences between the later Marx and Engels begins to look hopeless, and the reader turns back with relief to the Communist Manifesto and earlier works, on which these commentators devote almost all of their energies.

Once this shift of attention has taken place, the views of the later Engels have *in fact* come to obscure the tenets and indeed the importance of Marx's admittedly difficult critique of political economy, because Engels presented Marx's project and his important theoretical propositions as consistent with a materialism which he propounded. This materialism was defined (with certain ambiguities) in terms of Engels's view of natural science. He took natural science to be (potentially) universal in scope, inductive, causal and particularly concerned with the establishment of 'laws'. Thus by default Engels is granted the position he assumed – Marx's co-equal – in the role he adopted: 'scientific' theoretician. Both those 'conclusions' need examining; neither the word of Engels nor of commentators is sufficient to prove their truth. Moreover the assessment of the Marx–Engels relationship those 'conclusions' imply is profoundly ambivalent. If we take Engels's philosophising to stand for Marx's critique, his determinism to stand for Marx's 'guiding thread', and his interpretative context to stand for Marx's own, then who was *really*, as Engels put it, the 'first violin'?

1   The False Start

Karl Marx and Friedrich Engels first met in November 1842 when Marx was twenty-four and Engels just twenty-two. That meeting was not a success. Yet less than two years later their famous intellectual partnership was launched.

In considering any intellectual relationship we must look carefully at each partner's life and thought before they met in order to determine what each brought to the other, what experiences and ideas they had in common, and what they then accomplished together. With the Marx–Engels relationship we have further facts to explain: the false start, and the subsequent foundation of a partnership that lasted the thirty-nine years till Marx's death.

It is to Engels's intellectual biography that we must turn in order to explain the reversal in Marx's attitude between 1842 and 1844. This is fortunate, because the early Engels has received much less critical scrutiny than the youthful Marx. Though a more experienced and more extensively published writer than Marx, Engels was anxious for Marx's attentions as editor and polemicist, since it was Marx who commanded some notice and respect in the liberal politics of the Rhineland. The partnership was founded when Marx swung round from a curt dismissal to an enthusiastic collaboration, because of what Engels had undertaken in the interval between false start and firm friendship.

Marx's political development to the age of twenty-four, though remarkable, was not really at odds with his background. His father's household was that of a liberal lawyer, self-made, self-sufficient, but not rich; sceptical, inquiring,

1

respectful of the traditional arts and sciences, tolerant in religious affairs but never atheistic. Karl had an academic education based on the classics and liberal arts. Destined for university and a profession, he disappointed his father by taking up philosophy and history. His liberal politics extended to the serious consideration of socialism, atheism and revolution – the agenda, as it were, of the most radical French revolutionaries of the 1790s.

German intellectuals of Marx's day experienced those ideas through the works of G.W.F. Hegel, dead since 1831 but still a dominant, if highly ambiguous influence. Reactionary traditionalists and liberal-idealists alike found support in Hegel's philosophy, and it was with the radical camp that Marx aligned himself, drifting into journalism when an academic career became impossible for someone with his political sympathies. Liberal journalism was itself a precarious business; Marx's paper, the *Rheinische Zeitung* of Cologne, had to negotiate an impossible course between its civic backers and the various political enthusiasms of its contributors. Marx was the only person able or willing to take up the challenge, and even his considerable dialectical talents kept the paper going for only five further months. It was Marx as the new editor-in-chief of the *Rheinische Zeitung*, who gave Engels, a contributor to the paper since April 1842, a frosty reception in late November.

Engels's family background was commercial rather than professional, conservative rather than liberal and deeply religious rather than tolerantly sceptical. The Wupper Valley, where he grew up, was one of the first industrialised areas in Germany, and the Engels family had been mill-owners since the time of Friedrich's great-grandfather. Engels grew up in a Pietist household, where sober habits and Bible-reading reigned supreme in strict accord with the extreme Protestant sect. Pietist education was not intended to be intellectually stimulating, though a certain rationalism found its way into the grammar school, which Friedrich left at sixteen with good references in Latin, Greek ('the easier Greek prose writers'), French ('translates the French classics with skill') and German ('good, independent thoughts' and a 'commendable interest in the *history of German national literature* and the reading of the

German classics') (CW 2.584–5). Friedrich went into the family firm rather than to university, and he had his first taste of freedom when he went to work in Bremen a year later in the late summer of 1838.

It was then, even before he was eighteen, that Engels became a published poet and was already complaining about an editor who 'has completely destroyed 1) the main idea, 2) the cohesion of the poem'. 'As soon as I saw the changes', he wrote to his schoolfriends, the Graeber brothers, 'I became very angry and raged in a most barbaric fashion'. The 'main idea' was to contrast Bedouin tribesmen, even in their present humbled condition ('And freedom lost without a trace/They jump at money's beck and call'), with his audience in 'Parisian coats and vests' who were clearly despised by the poet. Yet Engels commented sceptically on his own talent: 'I shall also probably get a poem or two published in some journal because other fellows also do so who are just as big if not bigger asses than I am, and because my efforts will neither raise nor lower German literature' (CW 2.392–3, 394, 395–6).

Engels poured the same scorn on the liberal writers and critics of the day, the Young Germany movement of the 1830s, though he singled out Karl Gutzkow, editor of the Hamburg *Telegraph für Deutschland* as the most reasonable of all. Young Germany was 'a fine lot indeed!' (CW 2.411). The following spring Engels turned to more serious matters, writing to Friedrich Graeber in February 1839, 'I have just seen in the *Telegraph* a review of the poems of [J.C.F.] Winkler, the Barmen missionary... These extracts are really infinitely revolting'. 'Religious things', he continued 'are usually nonsense', (CW 2.415–16). The next month he wrote the most successful of his early works, the 'Letters from Wuppertal', published in Gutzkow's *Telegraph* in March/April 1839.

Engels protrayed his home district as a 'Zion of the obscurantists', linking religious fundamentalism, municipal fecklessness, poor taste, abysmal architecture, industrial pollution, poverty and exploitation in his survey. The River Wupper, bright red from effluent, guides the reader up the valley between smoky factory buildings and yarn-strewn bleaching yards. The workers of the valley occupied Engels's immediate attentions when he contrasted the effects of industrialisation on the populace with 'the wholesome, vigorous life of the people that exists almost everywhere in Germany'. While Engels's general view of the rest of Germany was somewhat naïve, or at least naïvely put, his report on the district he knew has the immediacy and power of an eyewitness account:

Every evening you can hear merry fellows strolling through the streets singing their songs, but they are the most vulgar, obscene songs that ever came from drunken mouths; one never hears any of the folk-songs which are so familiar throughout Germany and of which we have every right to be proud. All the ale-houses are full to overflowing, especially on Saturday and Sunday, and when they close at about eleven o'clock, the drunks pour out of them and generally sleep off their intoxication in the gutter. The most degraded of these men are those known as *Karrenbinder*, totally demoralised people, with no fixed abode or definite employment, who crawl out of their refuges, haystacks, stables, etc., at dawn, if they have not spent the night on a dungheap or on a staircase. By restricting the previously indefinite numbers of ale-houses, the authorities have now to some extent curbed this annoyance (CW 2.7–9).

About the reasons for this state of affairs Engels was utterly succinct: industrialisation. In particular he mentioned weavers, working at home, who 'dessicate their spinal marrow in front of a hot stove'; leather workers who were ruined physically and mentally after three years; children deprived of education and made victims of industrial accidents; and a range of industrial diseases, especially of the lungs. But what really occupied Engels was the peculiar culture that prevailed in the region, drawing strength from the conditions created by industrial development. Drunkenness, demoralisation and venereal disease, he noted, were rife among workers, who were also to be found miraculously converted (at times) to the fundamentalist, puritanical Christianity preached by itinerant and sometimes fraudulent revivalists. Engels described a related mysticism among mill-owners, on which he could speak with authority and about which there was rather more to say. The mysticism practised by the higher social strata was of a more doctrinaire sort, featuring 'savage intolerance' directed towards literature (particularly novels), opinion, amusements and dress (CW 2.9–12).

After reviewing the local preachers, their talents and relations with each other, Engels turned to the influence of
Pietism on other aspects of middle-class life – education and
the arts. Not surprisingly, he claimed that the Pietist spirit
pervades and corrupts every single aspect of life, typically
leading parents to identify intellectual progress with un-
believers. 'Anyone who plays whist and billiards, who can talk
a little about politics and pay a pretty compliment is regarded
as an educated man in Barmen and Elberfeld.' Local journal-
ists, writers and poets found little favour with Engels, who
concluded that the whole region is submerged in a sea of
Pietism and philistinism (CW 2.12–25).

Engels's analysis focussed on the bigotry, obscurantism and
anti-intellectualism of the property-owning classes of his
home district – obvious targets for a rebellious young man
who wanted more out of life than provincial monotony
and routine. What is striking about his 'Letters' is their
factuality, derived from his sharp observations, hunger
for knowledge and hatred of dogmatism. To this we can
attribute the inclusion of his comments on the environment
and working-class life. The fact that those comments come first
and are themselves linked with the scathing account of Pietism
is particularly interesting. While never claiming that industrialisation had in any way given rise to the cultural phenomena
that he deplored and disliked, Engels attributed the persistence
of Reformation sects to the needs and interests of factory
workers and owners alike, the former seeking an escape from
their miseries through religious enthusiasm and the latter
finding a ready exculpation for their role as employers and
their hypocritical politics:

The wealthy manufacturers have a flexible conscience and causing the
death of one child more or one less does not doom a Pietist's soul to
hell, especially if he goes to church twice every Sunday. For it is a fact
that the Pietists among the factory owners treat their workers worst
of all; they use every possible means to reduce the workers' wages on
the pretext of depriving them of the opportunity to get drunk, yet at
the election of preachers they are always the first to bribe their people
(CW 2.10).

'The article seems to have caused a sensation', Engels

commented accurately to his friend Friedrich Graeber later in
the month, adding: 'I am pleased with myself for not having
said anything in the article that I cannot prove' (CW 2.426–7).
In the same letter he wrote that under the influence of
rationalism and D.F. Strauss's *Life of Jesus* he had come to
doubt Christian orthodoxy. Strauss subjected the Gospels to
historical scrutiny, pointing out contradictions and discrepancies of the sort listed later by Engels: the '*Christi ipsissima
verba* of which the orthodox boast come out differently in every
gospel'. Engels's rationalism came forth in his belief that one
who seeks with all his heart to do as much good as possible
cannot be eternally damned, and even more strikingly in his
defence of the divine in man against the dead letter of Christian
orthodoxy (CW 2.426).

Having published so successfully in a paper identified with
the Young Germany movement, Engels modified somewhat
his assessment of the trend, writing on 6 May 1839 to the
Elberfelder Zeitung (which had taken a dim view of his 'Letters
from Wuppertal') that he had not 'the honour of belonging to
it', but signing himself to Wilhelm Graeber a few weeks later as
Friedrich Engels, Young German (CW 2.27, 452). His letter to
Friedrich Graber of 15 June summed up what he admired in the
movement – the search for truth and the eradication of
ignorance and compulsion in human affairs:

It is with me as with Gutzkow; when I come across someone who
arrogantly dismisses positive [i.e. rationalist] Christianity, then I
defend this teaching, which derives from the deepest needs of human
nature, the longing for salvation from sin through God's grace; but
when it is a matter of defending the freedom of reason, then I protest
against all compulsion. – I hope to live to see a radical transformation in religious consciousness of the world... Man is born
free, he is free! (CW 2.456).

Engels's religious doubts, his literary heroes, his journalism
and his politics were all linked in his espousal of feeling and
rationalism. His letters to Friedrich Graeber recorded the full
scope of his concerns:

True, feeling can confirm, but it can most certainly not furnish a
basis – that would be like wanting to smell with one's ears... The

Spirit of God may convince you through your feeling that you are a child of God – that is quite possible; but it most certainly cannot so convince you that you are a child of God through the death of Christ; otherwise feeling would be capable of thinking and your ears of seeing (CW 2.460–1).

'If you are consistent', he wrote to Graeber, 'you must consign him [the philosopher Friedrich Schleiermacher] to damnation, for he does not teach the word of Christ in your [Pietist] sense, but rather in that of Young Germany, of Theodor Mundt and Karl Gutzkow... and David Friedrich Strauss' (CW 2.462). Yet for Engels the struggles were not merely personal ones of religious conviction or intellectual battles in a pure realm of ideas, but real-world struggles in which individuals and groups, holding different beliefs, conflict with one another in personal, political and social terms:

What is rejected by science... should no longer exist in life either. Pietism may have been an historically justified element in the development of theology [but] it... should not now refuse to make way for speculative theology. It is only out of this latter that any certainty can be developed (CW 2.457).

These phrases from one of his published literary articles sum up Engels's manifesto: 'The struggle for freedom which produces all its manifestations – the development of constitutionalism, the resistance to the pressure of the aristocracy, the fight of the intellect against Pietism and of gaiety against the remnants of gloomy asceticism' (CW 2.32–3). Even a boat trip on the River Weser inspired him to pay private tribute in verse to the anniversary of the Revolution of July 1830 in France (CW 2.464).

However, revolutionary rhetoric went only so far. Engels retained real religious convictions (so far as we can tell from his correspondence with the Graebers), and he was similarly restrained in politics:

I protest against your insinuations that I have been giving the spirit of the times one kick after another in the hindquarters in order to speed its progress... On the contrary, when the spirit of the times comes along like a hurricane and pulls the train away on the railway line, then I jump quickly into a carriage and let myself be pulled along a little (CW 2.465).

He even took to explaining the 'operation of historical necessity during the period 1789–1839' to 'young fellows' in Bremen (CW 2.466). Evidently Engels had begun reading the works of Hegel, identifying himself with the radical Young Hegelian school of interpretation. 'Authority', he wrote, 'did not take the trouble to work its way through the abstruse forms of Hegel's system... but then, how could it have known that this philosophy would venture from the quiet haven of theory onto the stormy sea of actuality?' 'When authority protected Hegel,' Engels continued, 'when it elevated his teaching almost to a Prussian philosophy of the state, it laid itself open to attack, a fact which it now evidently regrets' (CW 2.143).

Thus Young Hegelianism was not a purely philosophical movement, as Engels noted:

... a few days ago I read in the paper that Hegelian philosophy has been banned in Prussia, that a famous Hegelian lecturer in Halle has been induced by a ministerial rescript to suspend his lectures and that it has been intimated to several junior Halle lecturers of the same colour (presumably [Arnold] Ruge, etc.) that they cannot expect appointments (CW 2.487).

For Engels, Hegel's work represented an application of reason to historical questions and a further triumph of science over superstition:

For I am on the point of becoming a Hegelian. Whether I shall become one I don't, of course, know yet, but Strauss has lit up lights on Hegel for me which make the thing quite plausible to me. His (Hegel's) philosophy of history is anyway written as from my own heart (CW 2.486).

For Engels, Young Hegelianism was not merely intellectual; it was deeply political:

Our future depends more than ever on the growing generation, for this generation will have to decide contradictions of ever-heightening intensity... We have a touchstone for the young in the shape of the new philosophy; they have to work their way through it and yet not lose the enthusiasm of youth... You need not therefore become Old Hegelians and throw around 'in and for itself', 'totality', and 'thisness', but you must not fight shy of the labour of thinking... In this sense the youth of today has indeed gone through Hegel's school, and in the heart of the young many a seed has come up splendidly from the system's dry husk. This is also the ground for the boldest confidence in the present; that its fate depends not on the cautious fear of action and the ingrained philistinism of the old but on the noble, unrestrained ardour of youth. Therefore let us fight for freedom as long as we are young and full of glowing vigour; who knows if we shall still be able to when old age creeps upon us! (CW 2.168–9).

Yet not every Young Hegelian won his praise. Karl Grün, a young poet, had very striking thoughts now and again, Engels said, but was often guilty of dreadful Hegelian phrases. 'What does this mean', Engels inquired: '"Sophocles is the highly moral Greece which lets its titanic outbursts break against the wall of absolute necessity. In Shakespeare the concept of absolute character made its appearance"' (CW 2.483–4).

Thus Engels's Hegelianism was of a discriminating kind: 'Through Strauss I have now entered on the straight road to Hegelianism. Of course, I shall not become such an inveterate Hegelian as [the conservative H.F.W.] Hinrichs and others, but I must nevertheless absorb important things from this colossal system' (CW 2.489).

The most important of the ideas absorbed by the young Engels was the Hegelian idea of God, which he identified as a modern pantheism, Hegel's principle that humanity and divinity are in essence identical (CW 2.489–90). This was the foundation stone of Young Hegelianism – if man and God are identical, traditional Christianity and the conservative politics of divine right, hierarchy, censorship and established churches must be overthrown. 'The enthusiastic, unshakable confidence in the idea, inherent in the New Hegelianism, is the sole fortress in which the liberals can find safe retreat whenever reaction gains a temporary advantage over them with aid from above'. 'We stand by our demand', he wrote, for 'a great united nation of citizens with equal rights!' (CW 2.143, 146).

Engels excoriated Friedrich Wilhelm III for his anti-consti-
tutionalism: 'his perjury is official... This same shabby,
rotten, goddamned king now has it announced through
[Bishop] Eylert [on 19 January 1840] that nobody is going to
get a constitution from him, for "All for one and one for all is
Prussia's principle of government"'. Declaring a mortal hatred
for the king and for almost every prince ruling between 1816
and 1830, Engels announced: 'I expect anything good only of
that prince whose ears are boxed right and left by his people
and whose palace windows are smashed by the flying stones of
the revolution' (CW 2.492–3).

So far as we know Engels actually threw no stones, but
continued his career as literary critic, publishing reviews on
Young German poetry and *belles lettres*, writing 'prose pieces
to practice my style', reading to a prospective publisher his
Odysseus Redivivus – an epic poem on the Greek revolt of
1821–5 against the Turks – and talking grandly of writing a
novel (CW 2.488). He wrote to his sister Marie, 'Recently, from
July 27th to 30th [1840], we celebrated the July revolution
which broke out ten years ago in Paris; we spent one evening in
the town-hall cellar and the others in Richard Roth's tavern...
There we drank the finest Laubenheimer in the world and
smoked cigars' (CW 2.501). Evidently this consoled him somewhat for the unsympathetic cultural environment of Bremen,
on which he reported, rather in the manner of the 'Letters from
Wuppertal', for a paper in Stuttgart. A few lines on social
conditions appeared near the end of the series – a description
of a visit to an emigrant vessel in the port of Bremerhaven:

All round the steerage runs a row of berths, several close together and
even one above the other. An oppressive air reigns here, where men,
women and children are packed next to one another like paving
stones in the street, the sick next to the healthy, all together. Every
moment one stumbles over a heap of clothes, household goods, etc;
here little children are crying, there a head is raised from a berth. It is
a sad sight; and what must it be like when a prolonged storm throws
everything into confusion and drives the waves across the deck, so
that the hatch, which alone admits fresh air, cannot be opened! And
yet, the arrangements on the Bremen ships are the most humane.
Everybody knows what it is like for the majority who travel via Le
Havre (CW 2.117–18).

Certainly Engels's facility in literary criticism dominates the 'Reports from Bremen', and there is little to suggest any real connection between the philistinism he bemoaned and the poor conditions for emigrant passage. This contrast with 'Letters from Wuppertal' may, of course, have several explanations: Bremen was a town of merchants rather than manufacturers; Engels may have judged what he wrote to be more suitable for his editor than the approach adopted in the earlier work; Engels's long experience in the Wuppertal was not matched by his brief acquaintance with the seaport he described. A new element in his analysis, though, was an enthusiastic description of an improvement in marine technology, a prognostication that the new equipment would have 'the greatest consequences', and a concluding generalization linking mankind, technology and emancipation:

A respected young local merchant has recently returned from London where he informed himself exactly about the equipment of the steamer *Archimedes* which, as you know, has a newly invented method of propulsion by an Archimedean screw... We will not have to wait long before we can reach New York from any part of Germany in a fortnight, see the sights of the United States in a fortnight, and be back home again in a fortnight. A couple of railways, a couple of steamships, and that's that; since Kant eliminated the categories of space and time from the sensory impressions of the thinking mind, mankind has been striving with might and main to emancipate itself from these limitations materially too (CW 2.128–9).

At the same time, in these journalistic works of 1840–1, Engels the economic liberal made an appearance, defending unlimited freedom and divisibility of landed property against the complicated restrictions present in most German states. Such restrictions, he argued, aggravate anomalies in agrarian relations – 'the development of big landowners into an aristocracy' – and create an absurd situation in which one generation has a right to dispose of the property of all future generations. Freeing of the land, Engels argued, restores 'the balance which in individual cases it may, of course, upset' since it generally allows no extremes to rise. The fettering of landed property, he wrote, 'works directly towards a revolution'; the revolutionary outcome, free trade in land, was compared by Engels to 'the surging ocean with its grand freedom' (CW 2.147).

In March 1841 Engels wrote to his sister, 'Thank God that I too am leaving this dreary hole [Bremen] where there is nothing to do but fence, eat, drink, sleep and drudge' (CW 2.529). Barmen, to which he returned, was described as 'pretty dry' except for 'some May wine or a student drinking bout' (CW 2.532). By August he was writing that 'nothing ever happens here', and in September he left for Berlin 'to do my duty as a citizen, i.e., to do what I can to evade conscription if possible' (CW 2.533–4).

Berlin, as it happened, offered Engels a great deal more than artillery training. He made up to some extent for the university education he never had by attending lectures at Berlin as a non-matriculated student, associating with such Young Hegelians as were in residence, pursuing his journalistic career and attending theatrical performances and poetry readings. He lived in private lodgings and was evidently not too burdened with the military duties which he satirised at length in letters to his sister Marie.

As usual Engels published an account of his impressions for readers distant from the scene; this time his medium was the *Rheinische Zeitung* of Cologne, to which he contributed the 'Diary of a Guest Student' in May 1842. Unlike his previous works on the Wuppertal and Bremen, the comments on Berlin, and particularly on the university, were highly favourable. The university, he wrote, was 'the most remarkable thing in Berlin', an institution which avoided the academic torpor of other German universities and was instead an arena of intellectual battles. Since it 'numbers representatives of all trends' on its staff, students get 'an easy, clear overall picture' of present-day thought, particularly the controversy over the new conservative refutation of Hegel offered by the philosopher Friedrich von Schelling. Hegel's work had become *that* dangerous.

Of all the lectures Engels attended, the most interesting, so he wrote, was P.K. Marheineke's on the introduction of Hegelian philosophy into theology. Engels chronicled the unusual applause when Marheineke reached his thinly veiled attack on Schelling as one who merely promised a refutation but did not keep his word. 'The grand, free vision with which Hegel surveyed the entire realm of thought and grasped the phenomena of life', Engels explained, 'is also Marheineke's inheritance' (CW 2.268–70). Some months previously Engels had attacked Schelling anonymously in Gutzkow's newspaper and in two substantial pamphlets. Initially he conceived the debate in national-historical terms:

Ask anybody in Berlin today on what field the battle for dominion over German public opinion in politics and religion, that is, over Germany itself, is being fought, and if he has any idea of the power of the mind over the world he will reply that this battlefield is the University, in particular Lecture-hall No. 6, where Schelling is giving his lectures on the philosophy of revelation (CW 2.181).

These terms broadened, a few paragraphs later, to the world-historical:

Judaism and Islam want to see what Christian revelation is all about; German, French, English, Hungarian, Polish, Russian, modern Greek and Turkish, one can hear all spoken together – then the signal for silence sounds and Schelling mounts the rostrum (CW 2.182).

Engels quoted Schelling at length and then attacked him for his view that philosophy has 'no claims whatever to any influence on the external world'. 'The good, naïve Hegel', Engels wrote, believed in the existence of philosophical results and the right of reason to enter into existence, to dominate being. To these colours Engels rallied the youth of Germany: 'in the end, one will be found among us who will prove that the sword of enthusiasm is just as good as the sword of genius' (CW 2.186–7).

Schelling and Revelation, though an anonymous pamphlet, brought Engels real recognition from the Young Hegelians. Arnold Ruge, Young Hegelian veteran of political discrimination in the universities and censorship in journalism, drew the attention of his readers in the newly founded *Deutsche Jahrbücher* to the controversial pamphlet and later, on learning the identity of its author, sought contributions from Engels himself.

In his pamphlet Engels reinvoked the tone of his anti-Pietist satires, characterising Schelling as a philosophical Messiah from whose hand Christians expected 'the fall of Hegelianism, the death of all atheists and non-Christians . . . by Easter 1842'. But everything turned out differently, Engels wrote, and Hegelian philosophy lives on in the young (CW 2.192).

The bulk of the pamphlet is remarkable for the clear, readable account it contains of the Young Hegelian movement. Engels began with the dying Hegel in 1831 in order to explain how disputes about his philosophical legacy had arisen, why these arguments were important, and who was involved. For someone who was, as he explained to Ruge later in 1842, 'young and self-taught in philosophy', the achievement is particularly impressive (CW 2.545).

'It was only after Hegel had died', Engels wrote, 'that his philosophy really began to live'. The commentaries by Hegel's pupils opened 'a straight, smooth road' to Hegel's philosophy which was seized upon by youth. The philosophy itself required reinterpretation, Engels claimed, because Hegel had himself confined 'the powerful, youthfully impetuous flood of conclusions from his teaching' within limits set by his own experience and personal opinions. His own political views after 1815 bore the stamp of the Restoration, and 'the world-historical necessity of the July revolution' (which Engels felt very deeply) never became clear to him. Hegel had failed, to some extent, to abstract himself from elements which were present in him as a product of his time and thus could not proceed accurately from pure thought alone. All inconsistencies and contradictions in Hegel's philosophy were traceable, according to Engels, to this dual historical and personal limitation on the free working of the Hegelian method. Hegel's independent, 'free-minded' principles were thus available to his pupils who were able then to jettison the 'cautious, even illiberal conclusions' (CW 2.195–6).

Hegel's philosophy of religion posed a real political dilemma: was it Christian or not? At first the radical Hegelians evaded the issue or attempted to keep 'the inevitable conclusions' esoteric to protect themselves from politically motivated allegations of atheism. At attack by Heinrich Leo in 1838 gave them 'clarity about themselves'. Engels traced the growth of philosophical atheism from Strauss's *Life of Jesus* (1835–6) to

Feuerbach's *Essence of Christianity* (1841) and the anonymous tract *Die Posaune* (1841) which 'demonstrates the relevant conclusions even in Hegel'. The last work, actually by Bruno Bauer, was singled out 'because it shows how often the bold, independent thinker in Hegel prevailed over the professor who was subject to a thousand influences'. Christianity, and even religion itself, have fallen, so Engels concluded, before the inexorable criticism of reason. Feuerbach's critique of Christianity, he wrote, 'is a necessary complement to the speculative teaching on religion founded by Hegel... Feuerbach reduces the religious categories to *subjective* human relations'. In this way he put the results achieved by Strauss to the real test and came to the same result, that the secret of theology is anthropology. It is the most sacred duty, Engels wrote in fine Young Hegelian style, 'of all who have followed the self-development of the spirit to transmit the immense result to the consciousness of the nation' (CW 2.196–7, 237–8).

Politically Engels traced the waning of official Prussian support for Hegelianism and the corresponding movement towards more overtly Christian and monarchical principles. Schelling was called to Berlin (from Munich) 'to ban the Hegelian teaching from its own field of philosophy' (CW 2.198). He attempted this, so Engels wrote, by arguing against the links proposed by Hegel between the reasonable, the necessary and the real: 'Hegel maintains that anything which is reasonable is also real; Schelling says, however, that what is reasonable is possible, and thus safeguards himself' (CW 2.200–2). Furthermore Schelling misunderstood Hegel's powerful dialectic, which Engels described in memorable terms as 'that inner motive force which constantly drives the individual thought categories... to ever new development and rebirth until they arise from the grave of negation for the last time as absolute idea in imperishable, immaculate splendour' (CW 2.206). And he had mistaken the relationship in Hegel of the Idea to nature and spirit: 'Schelling again conceives the Idea as an extramundane being, as a personal God, a thing which never occurred to Hegel. For Hegel the reality of the Idea is nothing but – nature and spirit' (CW 2.216).

After a lengthy rehearsal of Schelling's philosophising, Engels drew the sweeping conclusion that the 'irreconcilability of philosophy and Christianity has gone so far that even Schelling falls into a still worse contradiction than Hegel', who at least had a philosophy, 'even if the outcome was only an apparent Christianity'. Schelling, by contrast, produced 'neither Christianity nor philosophy', bringing home to one 'how weak are the foundations on which modern Christianity rests' (CW 2.235). In his critique Engels attempted to demonstrate that Schelling had smuggled 'belief in dogma, sentimental mysticism, gnostic fantasy into the free science of thinking' (CW 2.201). With a final Young Hegelian allegory, Engels indicated what he expected from such a free science: 'This is our calling, that we shall become the templars of this Grail, gird the sword round our loins for its sake and stake our lives joyfully in the last, holy war which will be followed by the thousand-year reign of freedom' (CW 2.239).

From straightforward philosophical analysis and political comment Engels turned once again to satire and travesty, publishing another anonymous pamphlet, *Schelling, Philosopher in Christ.* Its author appeared to be a strict Pietist, writing in the evangelical idiom familiar to Engels from his birthplace. Having damned Schelling as a critic, he evidently intended to bury him under unwelcome praise from a 'friend' whose philosophical views were frankly obscurantist: '*Schelling* has brought back the good old times when reason surrenders to faith' (CW 2.250). Engels's Pietist presented Schelling as a scourge to Berliners who interfered in government 'instead of leaving unto the King what is the King's business' (CW 2.260). In particular Schelling's mission was said to be the righteous destruction of 'the notorious *Hegel*' and his 'vile worldly wisdom' (CW 2.243). All rationalism came under attack, and Engels's Pietist waxed approving over Schelling's doubts concerning the scope of natural reason and the applicability of philosophical reasoning to reality. Schelling's 'negative philosophy', according to Engels and his Pietist, maintained that 'reason can only comprehend possibilities and nothing actual' (CW 2.248). Hegel, as interpreted by Young Hegelians, had blasphemously declared reason to be God and thus transcended Christianity and religion altogether (CW 2.250).

The conflict between Schelling and his conservative

Christian supporters on the one hand and Engels and the Young Hegelians on the other proceeded in the press. Some readers were even taken in by Engels's skill in parodying Pietism. But matters became rather more serious when Young Hegelians were dismissed from their posts for political reasons, most notably Bruno Bauer in late March 1842. Bauer's brother Edgar, and Engels contributed jointly to the protest movement by publishing *The Triumph of Faith*, a (supposedly) Christian epic relating how Bruno Bauer 'Seduced by the Devil, Fallen from the True Faith, Became Chief Devil and Was Well and Truly Ousted in the End' (CW 2.313). The pamphlet reproduced Engels's line on current academic and political disputes: Christians, armed with Faith, array themselves against the forces of reason who trace their lineage from Voltaire through Hegel, Strauss and Feuerbach. Bruno Bauer was portrayed, tongue-in-cheek, as an agent of the Devil, whose destruction marks the 'victory' of theology over philosophy, faith over reason, orthodoxy over free-thinking. More or less by name Engels and his co-author listed the Young Hegelians, including Ruge, Marx ('The Monster') and 'Oswald' (Engels's pen-name). In a caricature on his copy Engels named 'The Free', the Berlin group of Young Hegelians – Ruge, the brothers Bauer, and various others – though not Marx, the 'swarthy chap of *Trier*' mentioned in the poem (CW 2.336). At the work's conclusion Bauer's dismissal from Bonn University scatters 'The Free' in mock disarray:

But what's this floating down bathed in celestial light? What's making *Bauer* shake from head to foot with fright? It's just a little piece of parchment, strange to say. What might be written on it by the heavenly ray? It flutters down. At *Bauer's* feet it comes to rest. Shaking, he stoops and picks it up with heaving breast. – Why does the cold sweat on his brow spring so abundant? What does he murmur, stunned? He murmurs this – 'Redundant!' Hardly has Heaven's word from Hell's own mouth rung out, Before 'Redundant!' is the universal shout. The Free are horror-struck, the Angels filled with glee, The Free take flight, the Host pursues relentlessly. The Free are driven down to Earth in full confusion, That wicked folk shall all receive due retribution (CW 2.351).

This topical epic was excerpted in the German and Swiss

press, and it attracted comment from both conservatives and liberals. At the same time, summer 1842, Engels accepted Ruge's invitation to contribute to his Young Hegelian journal, which he did by reviewing Alexander Jung's 'Lectures on Modern German Literature'. In those articles Engels declared his wholehearted adherence to the Young Hegelian school – 'Strauss, Feuerbach, Bauer' – and announced that 'Young Germany has passed away'. His association with Gutzkow was definitively broken. This intellectual event was connected in Engels's characteristic fashion with contemporary doctrinal, philosophical and political controversy, albeit very generally conceived: 'The battle over principles is at its height, it is a question of life or death, Christianity is at stake, the political movement embraces everything' (CW 2.285). The catalogue of sins attributed to Jung and his fellow Young Germans (and 'writers of what is called Young Literature') is revealing in that it summarised the results of Engels's own intellectual and political development as a journalist, critic and student of philosophy. What he said about Jung is not traceable merely to partisanship – his adherence to one coterie rather than another – but to defensible criteria, intellectual and political, according to which Young Germany was found wanting.

Having accused Jung of being flabby, paltry, boring and cowardly in his published work, Engels came to the point by attacking Jung's interpretation of Hegel, for it was there that Jung revealed his deficiencies most tellingly. Jung was attacked for his academicism: 'he is up to his ears in a pile of books . . . and he labours to arrange the various items precisely and neatly into Hegelian categories'. More seriously his use of Hegelian categories revealed a faulty understanding of Hegel's philosophy which, according to Engels, led beyond mere assertions to 'the *reconciliation* of the subject with objective forces'. In that way Jung had missed the point of Hegel's work, obscuring its clear demand for real-world reconciliation with mysterious phrases and an unwarranted rejection of all extremes. These he considered evil, so he opted for a foggy conciliation and moderation expressed in vague, uncritical assertions (CW 2.284–7). For Jung's history of the Young German movement Engels substituted his own critical account, characterising its phases and then distributing praise and blame, depending on how closely a given writer approached the Young Hegelian view of Hegel and the current political struggle for liberalisation of the Prussian regime. The Young Germans initially found each other through an outward brilliance of style and an enigmatic mysticism in their slogans; their field was *belles-lettres*, which they conquered and divided; after that their inadequacy in matters of principle became apparent and the movement disintegrated into cliques, squabbles and disputes, becoming only a matter of personalities. Engels dismissed them as cranks: 'Liberal political principles differed among various personalities and the position of women gave rise to the most sterile and confused discussions... The fantastic form in which these views were propagated could only promote further confusion' (CW 2.290–1).

While rejecting Young Germany as a movement that had had its day, Engels reserved judgement on some of its adherents and registered considerable continuity in his own opinions, particularly in his view of Ludwig Börne (1786–1837), whom he had praised since 1839 for his political liberalism and for what Engels took to be his unrecognised closeness to the Hegelian outlook, in which Börne's 'direct, naïve' liberalism 'finds its completion'. Börne, Engels wrote, '*was a republican by his very nature*' whose link to Hegel was in considering life from the political point of view: 'Does not Hegel do the same? Is not for him, too, the state in its transition to world history, and therefore in the conditions of home and foreign policy, the concrete reality of the absolute spirit?' (CW 2.289).

As a final, damning criticism Engels linked Jung's views with Schelling's, writing that Jung had set himself up 'as a false prophet who predicts "a great birth of the positive"... which will conquer Strauss, Feuerbach and everything connected with them by the sword of the Lord'. In Young Hegelian fashion Engels characterised thought as positive and reality as, in a sense, negative, i.e. requiring criticism. 'Neo-Schellingian scholasticism', in his view, reversed this, characterising thought as negative ('because it develops instead of standing still', Engels commented sourly) and existent reality as positive ('an old ruined wall' for 'feeble ivy-like minds' to cling to, in Engels's Young Hegelian view of things). For Jung, Engels proposed the sort of obloquy favoured by liberals – frank criticism followed by a free, but well deserved obscurity:

> In the course of the above article he further discredits himself by indulging in the most trivial talk about the literary despotism of the liberals and defending his own freedom. Let him keep it; everyone will be quite ready to let him go blathering on for all eternity. But let him permit us to thank him for his support and to tell him honestly and frankly what we think of him (CW 2.293, 297).

Indeed, Engels's first contribution to the liberal *Rheinische Zeitung* was written in March 1842, about the same time that Marx transferred his efforts from Ruge's Young Hegelian *Deutsche Jahrbücher* to the same paper. Engels, as a Young Hegelian, wrote for both during 1842. His liberalism was of a simultaneously national and international variety linked 'to the whole of world history, and especially German history'. His article for the *Rheinische Zeitung* developed a contrast between south and north German liberalism, the former an eclectic, contradictory and ephemeral development of 1830 and the latter its worthy successor, distinguished by 'a high degree of consistency', 'definiteness' in demands, and 'a consonance of means and purpose'. Börne, unsurprisingly, was its precursor and prophet. South German liberalism made political convictions possible in Germany and awakened parliamentary life; it represented the gains of the July revolution in France. Engels's verdict, interestingly, was that it 'proceeded from practice to theory and failed; so let us begin the other way round and try to penetrate from theory into practice' (CW 2.266–7).

Engels's interests and ambitions had been shifting from literature and philosophy to more immediate political concerns since Bruno Bauer's dismissal from Bonn in March 1842; perhaps his contacts with the *Rheinische Zeitung* reinforced this trend. What is certain is that by the summer of 1842 Engels was writing on contemporary political events, as Marx had been doing since January, though his articles did not always achieve publication. Both commented critically on the Prussian censorship instructions of December 1841, and on other contemporary political debates: Marx on property law and poor relief, Engels on trial by jury and German unification. Marx's first published contribution to the *Rheinische Zeitung* was his long review of the 'Proceedings of the Sixth Rhine Province Assembly' on freedom of the press (written in April 1842 and published in May), and Engels contributed a short 'Critique of the Prussian Press Laws', written in June and published in July. Their independent verdicts on the evil effects of censorship and the ineffectual response of German politicians were virtually coincident. Marx wrote that a censored press has a demoralising effect, fostering hypocrisy, passivity and superstition since the government hears only its own voice (CW 1.167–8). Engels exposed the Prussian censorship as inconsistent and illogical, and declared his intention to 'awaken more than a little discontent and dissatisfaction with all obsolete and illiberal survivals in our state institutions' (CW 2.311).

Their journalistic efforts coincided again in response to an article by Moses Hess, published in May in the *Rheinische Zeitung*, on the more theoretical issue of centralisation and the modern state. Marx complained that Hess's Hegelian treatment had confused philosophy with imagination and that the author had substituted his own abstractions for real philosophy (CW 1.182–3). Marx's fragment lay unfinished and unpublished until 1927, however, whereas Engels's comments were written and published in September 1842. His framework was much more obviously Hegelian: 'The State is bounded on the one hand, by the individual and, on the other hand, by world history'. 'History', Engels wrote in a high Hegelian vein, 'has eternally had and will always retain the right to dispose of the life, the happiness, the freedom of the individual . . . it is the life of the species, and as such it is sovereign'. However, Engels distinguished in Young Hegelian terms between History and any particular state:

Thus, the English workers, who at present have to suffer bitter hunger, have indeed the right to protest against Sir Robert Peel and the English constitution, but not against history, which is making them the standard-bearers and representatives of a new principle of right. The same thing does not hold good for the state. It is always a particular state and can never claim the right, which mankind as a whole naturally possesses in its activity and the development of history, to sacrifice the individual for the general (CW 2.356–7).

Centralisation, Engels claimed, suffers from a contradiction: every state strives for centralisation, for that is its essence, yet this principle 'necessarily compels the state to reach out beyond itself' by claiming 'the authority and position that belongs only to history'. This contradiction, he argued, was manifested in the history of French absolutism, setting Paris over the provinces, giving rise to a disadvantageous disproportion in culture. 'Through Paris', he commented, 'France can indeed make revolutions and create free institutions at a single stroke, but she cannot keep them'. As a dedicated liberal Engels mourned the betrayal of the July revolution ('made by Paris alone') through the illiberal policies of François Guizot. The principles of popular sovereignty, a free press, independent juries and parliamentary government 'have practically been destroyed in France' (CW 2.355–9). On similar grounds Engels found the regime of the Prussian King Friedrich Wilhelm IV sadly wanting. He maintained the alliance between state administration and clerical reaction that was begun in the previous reign and had introduced his 'system' – a fully developed conservative romanticism requiring church attendance, Sunday restrictions, tightening of the laws on divorce (on which Marx later commented in the *Rheinische Zeitung*) and purging of theological faculties. His task was easy because he relied on the historical school of law, excoriated by Marx in August 1842 in the *Rheinische Zeitung* for 'positive, i.e. *uncritical*' arguments from wholly diverse authorities (CW 1.205). Friedrich Wilhelm IV, Engels wrote, did not recognise any universal, civic or human rights, only corporate rights, monopolies, privileges. In contrast, so Engels claimed, Prussian public opinion was now centring around two questions: representative government and freedom of the press. If that were gained, Engels foresaw a constitution, a representative system and annulment of the alliance with Russia (which was actually a factor in the demise of the *Rheinische Zeitung* the following year). Clearly he looked towards a more radical version of the July revolution (represented by ellipses in the following passage), but this time in Germany: 'Prussia's present situation closely resembles that of France before . . . but I refrain from any premature conclusions' (CW 2.360–7). That article was published abroad, in Switzerland.

As a Berlin resident Engels was at a considerable remove from the editorial disputes within the *Rheinische Zeitung*, in particular the running battle between its liberal backers, looking for reform propagated by a paper that would stay within the law, and Young Hegelian contributors given to philosophizing about history, freedom and revolution in terms that attracted the unwelcome attention of the authorities. Then a rival newspaper, in Marx's words, tried to 'saddle' the *Rheinische Zeitung* with 'The Free', about whom, he said, he did not know the slightest thing for sure. Marx continued gloomily to his associate Ruge:

It is fortunate that [Edgar] Bauer is in Berlin. He, at least, will not allow any 'stupidities' to be committed, and the only thing that disquiets me . . . is the probability that the insipidity of the Berliners will make their good cause ridiculous and that in a serious matter they will not be able to avoid various 'stupidities'. Anyone who has spent as much time among these people as I have will find that this anxiety is not without foundation (CW 1.390).

In November 1842, after he had assumed the editorship, Marx went into print against 'The Free' for 'compromising the cause and the party of freedom by their political romanticism, their mania for genius and boasting', and he attacked them for their 'frivolity', 'typically Berlin style of behaviour', 'insipid aping of the French clubs'. Sternly he concluded that 'rowdiness, blackguardism, must be loudly and resolutely repudiated in a period which demands serious, manly and sober-minded persons for the achievement of its lofty aims' (CW 1.287). Marx's editorial principle was clear: 'I consider it essential that the *Rheinische Zeitung* should not be guided by its contributors, but that, on the contrary, it should guide them' (CW 1.392). Just at the time that Engels, a charter member of 'The Free', turned up at the editorial office, Marx's campaign was in full swing. Ruge was given full details:

As you already know, every day the censorship mutilates us mercilessly, so that frequently the newspaper is hardly able to appear.

Because of this, a mass of articles by 'The Free' have perished. But I have allowed myself to throw out as many articles as the censor, for [Eduard] Meyen and Co. sent us heaps of scribblings, pregnant with revolutionising the world and empty of ideas, written in a slovenly style and seasoned with a little atheism and communism (which these gentlemen have never studied). Because of [Adolf] Rutenberg's complete lack of critical sense, independence and ability, Meyen and Co. had become accustomed to regard the *Rheinische Zeitung* as *their own*, docile organ, but I believed I could not any longer permit this watery torrent of words in the old manner. This loss of a few worthless creations of 'freedom', a freedom which strives primarily 'to be free from all thought', was therefore the first reason for a darkening of the Berlin sky (CW 1.393).

Meyen had dared to write to Marx, criticising him for his attitude to 'The Free' and his editorial policies. Marx said that he replied at once, listing the defects of their writings, 'which find freedom in a licentious, sansculotte-like, and at the same time convenient, form, rather than in a *free*, i.e., independent and profound, content' (CW 1.394). Marx's overall criticism of 'The Free' concerned their lack of political, intellectual and even empirical awareness:

I demanded of them less vague reasoning, magniloquent phrases and self-satisfied self-adoration, and more definiteness, more attention to the actual state of affairs, more expert knowledge. I stated that I regard it as inappropriate, even immoral, to smuggle communist and socialist doctrines, hence a new world outlook, into incidental theatrical criticisms, etc., and that I demand a quite different and more thorough discussion of communism, if it should be discussed at all. I requested further that religion should be criticised in the framework of criticism of political conditions rather than that political conditions should be criticised in the framework of religion, since this is more in accord with the nature of a newspaper and the educational level of the reading public; for religion in itself is without content, it owes its being not to heaven but to the earth, and with the abolition of distorted reality, of which it is the *theory*, it will collapse of itself. Finally, I desired that, if there is to be talk about philosophy, there should be less trifling with the *label* 'atheism' (which reminds one of children, assuring everyone who is ready to listen to them that they are not afraid of the bogy man), and that instead the content of philosophy should be brought to the people. *Voilà tout* (CW 1.394–5).

Marx's emphasis on expert knowledge and his insistence on a serious medium (not reviews or literary criticism) set him decidedly against 'The Free'. While his view of religion and his clear *political* perspective on the atheism question were strikingly like Engels's, the young Engels was undeniably more given to revolutionary rumblings and lofty Hegelian visions than Marx ever was. In his journalism Marx concerned himself with liberal provincial politics, the censor's attitude to a paper that might attract the label 'communist', and a properly serious approach to social change. As a result of Engels's association with 'The Free', Marx received him 'coldly', despite the coincidence of interests and views; both had taken social class into account in their works – Marx in his 'Thefts of Wood' and 'Mosel' articles, and Engels in his journalism on Wuppertal and Bremen (MEGA (Old Series), I/2, pp. lx–lxi). Neither man was the typical Young Hegelian *littérateur*, though Marx's strong sense of editorial vocation and practical involvement in local politics set him apart from – and at odds with – Engels, the talented writer, critic, satirist and eyewitness reporter. Engels was not, however, dropped from the *Rheinische Zeitung*. The paper continued to print contributions from its young correspondent in England, where Engels had gone to get acquainted with the overseas sector of the family cotton-spinning business. Marx's distaste for 'The Free' did not extend to any wholesale ban on their work, since in Engels he recognised a journalist with real power and a useful international perspective.

2 'By Another Road'

Though Engels did not really make Marx's acquaintance in November 1842, he did meet Moses Hess, revolutionary and communist, on an earlier visit to the *Rheinische Zeitung* in October. The extent to which Marx at this point had followed Hess down the road of revolutionary communism is obscure; if he had political sentiments beyond the liberal, Young Hegelian framework, they were carefully covered by his blunt concern to defend his paper from the censor and any outraged liberals who might be reading or backing it. This seems partly to explain Marx's reluctance to take overtly communist contributions; he commented later '... at that time when the good will "to go further" greatly outweighed knowledge of the subject, a philosophically weakly tinged echo of French socialism and communism made itself audible in the *Rheinische Zeitung*. I declared myself against this amateurism.' The remainder of the explanation lies in Marx's well-honed academic scepticism about 'French tendencies', i.e. communism, and his frank declaration that 'my previous studies did not permit me even to venture any judgement' (SW 180–1).

The *Rheinische Zeitung* was disbanded in March 1843, after harassment from the censor and provincial authorities. Marx's articles had been critical rather than overtly constructive or revolutionary. He exposed the trumph of private interests (of landowners, for example) over their tenants, of state officials over citizens, of censorship over informed public debate, of bureaucratic indifference over real feeling for the victims of economic circumstances. After the collapse of his paper (and his paid employment) Marx's private project was a manuscript critique of Hegel's *Philosophy of Right*, i.e. his social and political philosophy, including views on social class, employment, distribution of wealth, and other issues which might be described today as economic. In criticising Hegel's work Marx sought to destroy at least some of the more sophisticated arguments used by conservatives in defending the contemporary political and social order in Prussia, and at the same time to expose as clearly as possible the defining principles of that order itself. In that way, as critical analyst, Marx expected to get at the root of things, rather than merely to prescribe one administrative remedy or another. The thrust of Marx's critique was that piecemeal reform would inevitably fall victim to entrenched political forces so long as the system itself was still present in its fundamentals. His work on Hegel represents an exhaustive demolition of every Hegelian hope – conservative or liberal – for social peace and reconciliation.

But during the summer of 1843, while Engels was in England, Marx was not wholly preoccupied with private study. In company with Arnold Ruge and Moses Hess, he was attempting to set up an expatriate successor to the *Rheinische Zeitung* that would publish under more liberal circumstances and have a more significant political impact. As early as March 1843, when Marx drafted some 'Letters' later published by the group, he wrote very naturally as a revolutionary, which suggests that the studied liberalism of the *Rheinische Zeitung* did not represent the whole of his political viewpoint. Referring to the despotic character of the German state and to German shame before the French revolutionary tradition, Marx called the regime of Friedrich Wilhelm IV a 'ship full of fools', and predicted an 'impending revolution' (CW 3.133–4). In May he referred to Germany as a *dehumanised world* in which 'people who do not feel that they are human beings become the property of their masters', by which he meant 'hereditary masters', i.e. landowners and other propertied interests. 'Once one has arrived at the political world of animals', Marx wrote, 'reaction can go no farther'. The only possible advance would be 'the abandonment of the basis of this world and the transition to the human world of democracy' – 'a community of human beings united for their highest aims' (CW 3.137, 139).

Specifically, Marx predicted a 'rupture within present-day

society' caused by the 'system of industry and trade, of ownership and exploitation of people'. Elements of the communist outlook, as promulgated by Moses Hess for example, were certainly present. These included the humanism to be realised in a true community, the invocation of revolutionary spirit over animal-like passivity, the attention to what Marx called the 'theoretical existence of man' in religion, science and other aspects of intellectual life, and a vision of proletarians as particularly victimised and at the same time very promising revolutionary forces (CW 3.141, 143).

By September 1843, when Marx composed his last letter, Ruge and Hess had established offices for the new journal in Paris, and Marx, recently married, was looking forward to joining them. Marx's declared aim was to establish a new rallying point for truly thinking and independent minds, but he expected a pronounced seriousness in the enterprise. He would have no truck with any dogmatic abstraction which attempted to anticipate the world. 'Philosophers', he wrote ironically, have hitherto 'had the solution of all riddles lying in their writing-desks', and the world 'had only to open its mouth for the roast pigeons of absolute knowledge to fly into it.' His alternative method was '*ruthless criticism of all that exists*', in particular of communism when it was dogmatic, as in the 'actually existing communism' taught by Étienne Cabet, for instance, in his *Voyage to Icaria* (1842) and by Wilhelm Weitling, the first working-class German communist, in his *Mankind as It Is and Ought to Be* (1838) and *Guarantees of Harmony and Freedom* (1842). Weitling, like Hess, had learned his communism in Paris, and these works represented the French tendencies of which Marx was suspicious. His reservations were more methodological than overtly political; Marx was not the sort of liberal who rejected revolution, as we have seen. What he found objectionable in existing communism was a partial approach to social life, expecting too much from the mere abolition of private property. Marx implied that private property was itself so objectionable that it had 'infected' its communist antithesis. Communists were so far unsuccessful in thinking beyond the abolition of private property to the '*reality of the true human being*', who engages in important activities other than the mere appropriation of resources. Marx seemed to be suggesting that the abolition of private property under present political and cultural conditions would be disastrous and that alternative socialist doctrines, such as those put forward by F.M.C. Fourier (1772–1837) and Marx's near contemporary P.-J. Proudhon (1809–65), both of whom offered principles to guide communist communities, took inadequate account of the way that contemporary citizens had been moulded by a world in which private property ruled their lives. Refusing to get involved in French socialist debates, Marx kept his attention firmly fixed on Germany and on practical politics:

> ... we want to influence our contemporaries, paricularly our German contemporaries. The question arises: how are we to set about it? There are two kinds of facts which are undeniable. In the first place religion, and next to it, politics, are the subjects which form the main interest of Germany today. We must take these, in whatever form they exist, as our point of departure, and not confront them with some ready-made system (CW 3.142–3).

Some 'extreme Socialists', according to Marx, took the lofty view that discussion of current political issues, such as representation in government, was entirely beneath them. Marx declared that in 'analysing the superiority of the representative system over the social-estate system [as practised in Prussia], the critic *in a practical way wins the interest* of a large party'. Marx's method was to take '*real* struggles' and then to engage in criticism, rather than to follow the dogmatic method practised by communists and socialists when they pronounced their new principles and then stated, in Marx's dramatised account: 'Here is the truth, kneel down before it!' (CW 3.144).

The real struggles that Marx suggested as his first targets were religion and politics as perceived in Germany, where they embodied 'mystical consciousness'. It was the critic's vocation to make plain the truth. This Marx referred to as the 'reform of consciousness', explaining to the world 'the meaning of its own actions' and 'awakening it out of its dream about itself'. Marx's academic scepticism was allied to his feel for practical politics – revolution could never be as simple as communists had suggested nor as manageable as socialist system-building had implied. Practical revolutionary activity, he suggested, grows out of the mundane political conflicts in which people are already engaged and, conversely, an *a priori* or even messianic approach which disdained contemporary politics was doomed, in Marx's view, to fail. In addition he presented a balance and dialogue in the relationship between theorist and citizen that eluded some of his contemporaries, who were more intellectually aloof when they forebore to engage in debates they had not generated themselves (CW 3.144).

There is virtually nothing in the methodology and the politics of these early 'Letters' that contradicts Marx's later work. He was never, for example, against a reform of consciousness, the stated motto of 1843. Then, as later, he objected to any pretence that reform came from a *dogmatic* consciousness alone, or that consciousness was itself the whole of human life or its defining element. The reality of human life for Marx, in 1843 as later, embraced a complexity in practical and theoretical activities that could not be wished away. Within that complexity he turned his critical attention to demystifying 'legal relations' (e.g. property law), 'forms of state' (e.g. representative government), religion, and science (e.g. social science such as political economy) in order to promote political change (CW 3.143–4; SW 181).

In his formative years 1842–43, Marx was undoubtedly a liberal who supported a free press, representative institutions and freedom of thought and opinion, particularly with regard to the criticism of religion. To be a liberal in that sense was obviously to be in radical opposition to a monarchical regime dedicated to hierarchy, obedience, Christianity, paternalism and the division of society into favoured and less favoured estates. Social class was therefore an issue that neither side could successfully ignore, however obscurely the matter was put, and, because of the radical disagreement between the two sides on fundamental principles, reform and revolution were not readily distinguishable. Hence we may conclude that Marx was at least as revolutionary as many more conventional liberals; given the vehemence with which he wrote in the *Rheinische Zeitung* and his frank comments on revolution after the paper closed, it seems certain that he was also a revolutionary in much more than the minimal sense.

Was he also a socialist and communist whose merely liberal articles in the *Rheinische Zeitung* reflected a certain strategic self-censorship? If so, was the liberalism in those articles in some sense insincere, or alternatively was it sincere but incomplete as a summary of all that the author believed in? Marx was evidently not a socialist in the conventional sense of the time, that is one who adhered to doctrine found in the works of writers such as Cabet, Fourier and Proudhon. Nor was he a thorough-going communist: one who looked specifically to working-class revolution to usher in a new age of truly human cooperation. Socialism and communism at this time had as many definitions as practitioners, and the distinction I have just offered was not one which all writers would have accepted then, nor is it one which would allow us to denominate any given radical as definitely socialist rather than communist or *vice versa*. Yet it was Hess and Weitling who made working-class revolution an issue in German radical politics, and it was with that camp that Marx allied himself when he opted to go to Paris at the end of Octobei 1843.

Even that group, however, was subjected by Marx to the ruthless criticism he favoured, and no propositions were taken on trust. His association with the communist group, rather than with more moderate Germans, who were typically (rather like Feuerbach) more concerned with philosophical debates pursued in an academic way, is significant. Yet it is also unsurprising, given Marx's obvious interest in disadvantaged groups in German society. In his experience, however, these were peasants and smallholders; industrial workers were somewhat outside his ken, although not therefore excluded in advance of any consideration of their circumstances. Nor were they particularly favoured merely because Hess, who at this period looked to the English working-class, had announced that they were an essential element of European revolution. I think it plain that Marx at this time considered proletarians to be disadvantaged, the victims of absolute monarchy allied with the propertied classes in Germany and similarly victimised by more modern representative regimes. His declared methodology in the *Rheinische Zeitung* – engagement with the local political issues that involved or would involve his readership – makes his preferential attention to the problems of German peasants and small-holders explicable.

Though Marx refrained from attacking the monarchy directly, for obvious reasons, his withering criticism of its institutions and administration, particularly when the interests of the poor were at stake, leaves little doubt that his few positive suggestions, e.g. freedom of the press, do not represent the sum total of what he envisaged as an alternative social order. In fact it is difficult to imagine, given what he said about the role of the free press in promoting real political dialogue among citizens, that the economic needs of those citizens were irrelevant. Indeed, the fact that Marx described them explicitly as '*citizens of the state*' indicated his position, since from the regime's point of view they were no such thing, nor could they ever conceivably be citizens in the full egalitarian sense envisaged by Marx. The press, Marx wrote, can 'mitigate the distress' of the Mosel region, for example, 'by dividing the feeling of it among all'; moreover 'an exceptional freedom of the press' was required 'to satisfy the existing need' which was detailed in economic terms (CW 1.348–9).

The editors of the *Deutsch-Französische Jahrbücher* (as Marx and Ruge called their new journal) received the 'Outlines of a Critique of Political Economy' from Friedrich Engels in November 1843. The effect on Marx was overwhelming. Here was a guide to the most precise social theory available, the science of political economy, that quite eclipsed Hegel's synthetic (and idiosyncratic) treatment of economic life in the *Philosophy of Right*, now twenty years out of date anyway. Evidently Marx had already made the connection between Hegel's work on civil society and the subsequent search for its anatomy in political economy, because his comments on Engels's article appear in the fifth of his excerpt notebooks, which date from the beginning of his stay in Paris; notes on Adam Smith's *Wealth of Nations* (1776) appear in the second and third.

Engels's critical attack on selected political eco-nomists – Smith, David Ricardo, J.R. MacCulloch, T.R. Malthus and others – coincided with Marx's programme of research. More importantly for Marx, it represented a serious, systematic criticism of another 'mystical consciousness' (the apologetic side of political economy), obscuring the real-world struggles through which a practical revolutionary, interested in what Marx carefully described as 'possible communism', might begin to assist mankind (CW 3.143, 144, 610 n. 136). That Marx continued to accept contributions to the *Rheinische Zeitung* from Engels after the cool reception in November 1842 argues his interest in an investigation into Hess's hypothesis that the English working-class had a special role to play in the European revolutionary movement. Engels, as we have seen, had had his eye on the condition of industrial workers since the sensational 'Letters from Wuppertal' of 1839, and he had visited England, including the north, very briefly in 1840, so his views on English working-class politics, however stimulated by his contact with Hess the famous communist, were hardly an application of newly received ideas from a charismatic mentor. Engels's articles for the *Rheinische Zeitung* of late 1842 argued that Chartism was essentially a working-class movement whose interests set it apart from reformists among the middle-classes. At the same time Engels cast doubt on the Chartists' peaceful strategy for that very reason: the middle-class would never 'renounce its occupation of the House of Commons by agreeing to universal suffrage' (CW 2.368–9). In his next article Engels argued the truth of the communist hypothesis that the English working-class has a revolutionary mission by virtue of its utter dependence on the economic circumstances of industrial capitalism:

For although industry makes a country rich, it also creates a class of unpropertied, absolutely poor people, a class which lives from hand to mouth, which multiplies rapidly, and which cannot afterwards be abolished, because it can never acquire stable possession of property. And a third, almost a half, of all English people belong to this class (CW 2.373).

Crucial to Engels's analysis was his view that the modern industrial nation is inherently subject to a 'contradiction' which admits of no solution:

Further, a natural consequence of the premises of the industrial state is that, in order to protect the source of its wealth, it has to keep out the industrial products of other countries by means of prohibitive import duties. But since the home industry raises the prices of its products in step with the import duties on foreign products, this makes it necessary also to increase import duties constantly, in order that foreign competition shall continue to be eliminated, in accordance with the accepted principle. Hence the result would be a two-sided process going on to infinity, and this alone reveals the contradiction inherent in the concept of the industrial state (CW 2.372).

Significantly, Engels claimed that his argument was not wholly based on what he called 'these philosophical categories' but could also be confirmed by direct observation of the existing interests of foreign and domestic producers and consumers and the resulting political pressures. The next result for England, so Engels claimed, would be a steady contraction of home industry from which the working-class would suffer disproportionately:

The slightest stagnation in trade deprives a considerable part of this class of their bread, a large-scale trade crisis leaves the whole class without bread. When such a situation occurs, what is there left for these people to do but to revolt? By its numbers, this class has become the most powerful in England, and woe betide the wealthy Englishmen when it becomes conscious of this fact (CW 2.372-3).

Engels claimed to see the awakening of the working-class revolutionary perspective in the strikes of August 1842, though he admitted that they were essentially unorganised, non-revolutionary in their ultimate respect for the legal order and inchoate in their aims. Continental assessments, presumably communist ones, which saw proletarian revolution rising in England were quite premature, Engels argued, though in the longer term he predicted that the 'dispossessed have gained ... the realisation that a revolution by peaceful means is impossible' and that their only hope would be 'a forcible abolition of the existing unnatural conditions'. Revolution was 'inevitable', he argued, because the country's economic prospects were such that 'there cannot fail to be a general lack of food among the workers ... and then fear of death from starvation will be stronger than fear of the law' (CW 2.373-4).

At the same time Engels argued that England was behind the

continent in intellectual progress; presumably he meant the Young Hegelian philosophy in Germany and the socialism, communism and revolutionary tradition in France. He denigrated English freedom as purely formal and deplored the enduring power of feudalism and its immunity from attack in actual fact and in public opinion. In his articles for the *Rheinische Zeitung* Engels had evidently moved somewhat beyond the perspective of Moses Hess in his uncompromising view that revolution would be violent and in his low opinion of the Englishman's allegedly practical, down-to-earth outlook on life. Moreover, he declared that 'it will be interests and not principles' (as Hess was wont to imply) 'that will begin and carry through the revolution'. Principles have a role to play though, since they 'develop only from interests', something which 'the obstinate Briton' does not understand. The British outlook, according to Engels, was that 'so-called material interests' (a phrase repeated by Marx in his 1859 autobiographical sketch) do not operate independently in history; principles, which control 'the threads of historical progress', must be taken into account. So in Engels's view stagnation in trade was not merely some temporary phenomenon of limited significance but part of a complex historical development in which working-class political consciousness rises against the ruling classes. That historical view, in moving beyond 'surface appearance' to expose 'the basis' (terms adopted by Marx, once again, in his later works), was part of the continental and particularly German intellectual progress still alien to 'the national English standpoint' (CW 2.370–1, 374).

Marx's stated methodology of 1843 – analysis of contemporary political issues, ruthless criticism of existing analytical categories such as those used by politicians and philosophers, avoidance of *a priori* pronouncements and doctrines, clear connections between political manoeuvres and economic interests, and a drive towards dialogue between participant and theorist – were all reproduced in Engels's works of late 1842 with stunning clarity. Previous works by both Marx and Engels anticipated this, but did not exhibit it exactly, for a variety of reasons: the medium and audience for any given work, the character of the political issues under discussion, the intentions of the author when writing (e.g. some of Engels's early pieces were frankly for entertainment), and the developing skill and perspective of the author himself. Overnight conversions and imitative discipleship are not helpful categories in examining the early intellectual development of Marx and Engels.

Engels's 'Outlines of a Critique of Political Economy' was brilliant, as Marx later said (SW 182). It displayed a unity of purpose, systematic approach and clarity of discrimination that set it apart from his work up to that time. However good his journalism and laudable (from Marx's point of view) his investigations into the socialist movement in Britain, Engels must have risen uniquely in Marx's estimation to a level of esteem quite beyond that accorded to editorial colleagues such as Ruge. Engels's essay was a clear departure in subject matter – contemporary political economy – from previous Young Hegelian efforts, and it was moreover an area in which Germans were generally weak. Young Hegelians and communists alike were at best muddled and at worst completely ignorant of this important field dominated by the British and French. The informative yet ruthlessly critical approach must have appealed immensely to Marx, who was, with typical thoroughness, only just beginning to tutor himself in the subject with a long course of reading, and even that was mostly in translation.

Most remarkably, Marx's manuscript notes on Engels's essay prefigured the course of his lifework in a few compressed phrases written early in 1844. He began with '*Private property*'. This summed up the apparent source of the social, economic and political inequalities about which he had written for the *Rheinische Zeitung* in 1842–43, and it pointed to his interest in socialist attacks on the institution. It also indicated for Marx the need to *investigate* the communist cure-all, which was the abolition of private property in favour of 'common property', as Engels put it in an article written in October/November 1843. In that article he implied that 'Dr. Marx' had been party to this conclusion as early as autumn 1842, the beginning of his editorship of the *Rheinische Zeitung* and a year before he set up in the more obviously proletarian surroundings of Paris and declared his explicitly revolutionary sympathies for the 'class with *radical chains*' in an article (written at the end of 1843) for the *Deutsch-Französische Jahrbücher* (CW 3.186, 375, 406). The immediate consequence of private property, Marx continued, was 'trade' as it takes place under contemporary capitali: . arrangements – 'a *direct* source of gain for the trader'. 'The next category to which trade gives rise', he concluded, 'is *value*' (CW 3.375). In effect his political commitment (to an economic, social and political system alternative to capitalism and the inegalitarian regimes supporting it), his subject matter (political economy), his programme of research (a critical account of its categories) and even his starting point in presentation (theory of value *via* the concept of the commodity) were strikingly and uniquely stated by Marx, once he had read Engels's 'sketch on the criticism of the economic categories'. Marx even noted later that he 'maintained a constant exchange of ideas by correspondence' with Engels, though nothing survives nor is mentioned elsewhere by either until their exchange of letters in October 1844. This correspondence began after the two had spent ten days together in Paris on Engels's return to the continent at the end of August (SW 182). By then the partnership was founded.

Certain aspects of the Young Hegelian methodology were prominently displayed in Engels's 'Critique of Political Economy', later the subtitle of Marx's *Capital*. As in that work the emphasis was on a conceptual analysis that precedes empirical investigations. The author trusts such research would corroborate the initial theoretical work, rather in the manner of scientific hypothesis and subsequent tests. In his critique Engels used familiar Hegelian apparatus, uncovering 'the contradiction', in this case the one introduced by the free-trade system, and then bringing out 'the consequences of both sides'. Marx's *Capital* was in effect a much elaborated specification of the contradiction discussed by Engels in his 'Outlines'. As in Marx's attempt to delve beneath the surface phenomena of the capitalist economy, Engels proposed to do what the political economists had failed to do, namely examine their theoretical premises, the same premises that 'begot and reared the factory system and modern slavery, which yields nothing in inhumanity and cruelty to ancient slavery'. Engels accused the most recent political economists – MacCulloch and James

Mill – of the worst sophistry and hypocrisy in evading the true consequences of private property. The science of political economy was conceived by Engels as itself an emanation of the merchants' mutual envy and greed, bearing 'on its brow the mark of the most detestable selfishness' (a metaphor, possibly borrowed from the Book of Revelation, later adopted by Marx in his discussion of value and money in *Capital*) (CW 3.418–21).

The overall historical framework in Engels's 'Outlines' was more overtly and more controversially of the Hegelian school, since he traced a process of revolutionary social transformation through the resolution of 'contradictions'. This view is less easily identifiable in Marx's works, though there are traces of it in some of his more apocalyptic accounts of proletarian revolution and the end of the capitalist system. Working from the recent past, Engels identified eighteenth-century revolutions as 'one-sided and bogged down in antitheses'. Economically the age did not get beyond 'antithesis' and 'sham philanthropy'; in politics the social contract was counterposed to divine right, and republic to monarchy; in philosophy abstract materialism was set in opposition to abstract spiritualism and Nature elevated over Man, just as the Christian God confronted humanity as humiliated and contemptible sinners. Engels's communism undermined those religious and philosophical contradictions by using Feuerbach's critique of Hegelian idealism from the *Essence of Christianity* and elsewhere. His work was praised by Engels in the attacks on Schelling of early 1842 and in other articles; Feuerbach was later specifically cited as an important critical figure in Engels's own history of the Young Hegelian period, his *Ludwig Feuerbach and the End of Classical German Philosophy* (CW 3.419–20, SW 592).

The economic and political contradictions were also tackled within Engels's communist outlook when he took the *validity of private property* to be the key question. His view proceeded 'from a purely human, universal basis'; only from that basis could the 'conceptual confusion' and 'double-tongued logic' of rival schools of political economy be sorted out. Hence 'the English Socialists' have long since 'proved practically and theoretically' that, as opponents of private property, they are in a position to settle economic questions more correctly than are political economists whether free-traders or monopolists. Engels argued that analysis would in any case reveal free-traders to be more inveterate monopolists than their rivals the mercantilists. He was however less informative on the exact resolution of the political contradictions he had identified; 'the struggle of our time', he said gnomically, will become 'a universal human struggle'. Even more obscure was his use of a quasi-Hegelian doctrine of historical necessity:

It was necessary for the theory of private property to leave the purely empirical path of merely objective inquiry and to acquire a more scientific character which would also make it responsible for the consequences, and thus transfer the matter to a universally human sphere. It was necessary to carry the immorality contained in the old economics to its highest pitch, by attempting to deny it and by the hypocrisy introduced (a necessary result of that attempt) (CW 3.419–421).

Once past his introduction, Engels posed the topic which Marx took up in the opening sentence of *Capital*: 'The wealth of those societies in which the capitalist mode of production prevails, presents itself as "an immense accumulation of commodities"...' [the quotation is from Marx's earlier published work of 1859, *A Contribution to the Critique of Political Economy*] (CAP 1.43). In a sense Marx's own exposition provided the 'meaning' Engels called for early in his 'Outlines':

The term national wealth has only arisen as a result of liberal economists' passion for generalisation. As long as private property exists, this term has no meaning. The 'national wealth' of the English is very great and yet they are the poorest people under the sun. One must either discard this term completely, or accept such premises as give it meaning (CW 3.421).

Engels then analysed trade in terms that were rather nearer the surface phenomena of real economic practice than those considered in Marx's later published critique. This was unsurprising, given Engels's practical experience as a businessman. In language that appeared later in the Communist Manifesto, Engels assessed the impact of capitalist trade in spreading civilisation and fraternity among peoples, and dissolving nationalities, while at the same time subjecting the whole earth to '*one* great, basic monopoly, property', intensifying enmity between individuals and destroying the family. All of this he traced, as in his methodology of late 1842, to a principle, the separation of interests of buyer and seller, the very basis of the free-trade system. 'Once a principle is set in motion', he concluded, 'it works by its own impetus, through all its consequences'. This was much as Marx argued later in deducing the socio-economic consequences of the law of value in *Capital*, in which he specified how Engels's separation arises. Engels, however, concluded more grandly that even the 'egoistical reasoning' of the political economists 'forms but a link in the chain of mankind's universal progress' (CW 3.423–4).

Similarly Engels's analysis of value revolved around the surface concept 'price', rather than Marx's more deeply theoretical investigation of the value – labour relationship, merely mentioned by Engels (in inverted commas) as the '"source of wealth"' (CW 3.431). The remaining categories of the analysis, 'the rent' for land, 'the capital with its profit' and 'the wages' for labour, were the three adopted by Marx in writing the *Economic and Philosophical Manuscripts* of April–August 1844: 'Wages of Labour', 'Profit of Capital' and 'Rent of Land' (CW 3.235, 246, 259, 427). Engels was not, in his short work, about to launch into such a ruminative, excerpt-heavy investigation of what the major political economists had said on these subjects. Much more interestingly he appealed to natural science in its technological applications in industry as a category more appropriate to an analysis which goes 'beyond the division of interests as it is found with the economist' (CW 3.427–8). In doing so he prefigured the 'premises' of the manuscript *German Ideology* (of 1845–6), a work to which Marx attributed particular significance in his own autobiographical sketch of 1859. These premises are presupposed in all Marxian analysis.

The first premise of all human history is, of course, the existence of living human individuals. Thus the first fact to be established is the physical organisation of these individuals and their consequent relation to the rest of nature... Men can be distinguished from animals by consciousness, by religion or anything else you like. They themselves begin to distinguish themselves from animals as soon as they begin to *produce* their means of subsistence (CW 5.31).

Engels's earlier comments in the 'Outlines' derived much the same result from a critical inquiry into the characteristic assumptions of political economists, which Engels found mystificatory and deficient:

According to the economists, the production costs of a commodity consist of three elements: the rent for the piece of land required to produce the raw material; the capital with its profit; and the wages for the labour required for production and manufacture. But it becomes immediately evident that capital and labour are identical, since the economists themselves confess that capital is 'stored-up labour'. We are therefore left with only two sides – the natural, objective side, land; and the human, subjective side, labour, which includes capital and, besides capital, a third factor which the economist does not think about – I mean the mental element of invention, of thought... the advances of science... We have, then, two elements of production in operation – nature and man, with man again active physically and mentally (CW 3.427-8).

Engels's few sentences are not themselves 'the brilliant germ of the new world outlook' that he detected in Marx's *Theses on Feuerbach* of early 1845 (SW 585). They were however part of the inspiration on which Marx drew in his own *Economic and Philosophical Manuscripts* that were written in 1844, just after the notebooks on political economy which contain his résumé of Engels's 'Outlines'. These now famous manuscripts of 1844 display an intermediate stage of conceptual elaboration between Engels's critique of the economists' basic categories, and the much crisper 'premises' of *The German Ideology*. Here is what Marx wrote in 1844:

The life of the species, both in man and in animals, consists physically in the fact that man (like the animal) lives on inorganic nature... The universality of man appears in practice precisely in the universality which makes all nature his *inorganic* body – both inasmuch as nature is (1) his direct means of life, and (2) the material, the object, and the instrument of his life activity (CW 3.275-6).

Marx's 'premises' of 1845-6 arose, so I have argued, as his

critical approach to private property moved from the consideration of social and political philosophy to the more specific
propositions of the political economists concerning the
production of privately distributed 'wealth'. These 'premises'
underlie all his later work. His 'guiding thread' of 1859 makes
little sense without them, and the purpose of *Capital* within his
larger plans cannot really be grasped in any other terms.

In the *Theses on Feuerbach* the category 'production', which
also figures large in the 1844 manuscripts and *The German
Ideology* and in Engels's 'Outlines', was subsumed into the
more general, more abstract *'sensuous human activity, practice'*,
'practical human-sensuous activity' and 'human practice' –
terms more relevant than 'production' in a response to
the abstractions of Feuerbachian philosophy (CW 5.3–5).
In the very late *Ludwig Feuerbach and the End of Classical
German Philosophy*, an overtly philosophical work, Engels
attributed a special significance to Marx's *Theses* which seems
somewhat misplaced compared to the precision of *The German
Ideology*, and unduly denigratory of his own work in the
inspirational 'Outlines' (SW 585).

Marx included the 'Outlines' in the notes to *Capital* no less
than four times, most strikingly when he revealed, early in the
work, his own answer to the riddle of the trade crisis posed in
graphic terms by Engels:

The law of competition is that demand and supply always strive to
complement each other and therefore never do so ... The economist
comes along with his lovely theory of demand and supply, proves to
you that 'one can never produce too much', and practice replies with
trade crises ... What are we to think of a law which can only assert
itself through periodic upheavals? (CW 3.433–4).

Besides resolving the cause of crises (to his own satisfaction)
Marx also managed to pin down Engels's metaphor in this
passage from *Capital*:

... in the midst of all the accidental and ever fluctuating exchange-
relations between the products, the labour-time socially necessary for
their production forcibly asserts itself like an over-riding law of
Nature. The law of gravity thus asserts itself when a house falls about
our ears (CAP 1.80).

Certain conclusions in the 'Outlines' were mirrored in Marx's vision in *Capital* of the conscious regulation of production 'in accordance with a settled plan', and in these words on 'the knell of capitalist private property' strategically placed near the end of the very long volume:

Along with the constantly diminishing number of the magnates of capital, who usurp and monopolise all advantages of this process of transformation, grows the mass of misery, oppression, slavery, degradation, exploitation; but with this too grows the revolt of the working-class, a class always increasing in numbers, and disciplined, united, organised by the very mechanism of the process of capitalist production itself (CAP 1.84, 715).

Engels's views of late 1843 are virtually identical:

If the producers as such knew how much the consumers required, if they were to organise production, if they were to share it out amongst themselves, then the fluctuations of competition and its tendency to crisis would be impossible. Carry on production consciously as human beings – not as dispersed atoms without consciousness of your species – and you have overcome all these artificial and untenable antitheses. But as long as you continue to produce in the present unconscious, thoughtless manner, at the mercy of chance – for just so long trade crises will remain; and each successive crisis is bound to become more universal and therefore worse than the preceding one; is bound to impoverish a larger body of small capitalists, and to augment in increasing proportion the numbers of the class who live by labour alone, thus considerably enlarging the mass of labour to be employed (the major problem of our economists) and finally causing a social revolution such as has never been dreamt of in the philosophy of the economists (CW 3.434).

Characteristically Engels also went beyond what Marx, in his critical reticence, was ever willing to say about the social relations of the future. Marx was little given to favourable comments on other socialists, possibly for fear of being saddled with the job of defending ideas he could not wholly endorse, and he certainly never recommended their views on future society in such a sweeping way:

The community will have to calculate what it can produce with the means at its disposal; and in accordance with the relationship of this productive power to the mass of consumers it will determine how far it has to raise or lower production, how far it has to give way to, or curtail, luxury. But so that they may be able to pass a correct judgement on this relationship and on the increase in productive power to be expected from a rational state of affairs within the community, I invite my readers to consult the writings of the English Socialists, and partly also those of Fourier.

Subjective competition – the contest of capital against capital, of labour against labour, etc. – will under these conditions be reduced to the spirit of emulation grounded in human nature (a concept tolerably set forth so far only by Fourier), which after the transcendence of opposing interests will be confined to its proper and rational sphere (CW 3.435).

After his association with Marx had begun in earnest, however, Engels displayed a more critical approach to those whom Marx considered utopians and to what Marx dismissed in 1873 as 'receipts... for the cook-shops of the future' (CAP 1.26).

The remainder of Engels's article is almost a conspectus of volume one of Marx's *Capital*, once the theories of value, surplus value and exploitation are established. Engels considered unemployment and took to task the theory of overpopulation found in Malthus (Marx footnoted Engels's work on this point at CAP 1.594); like Marx, he attributed great importance in the dynamic of capitalist development to technological change through the application of science. Engels dismissed glib theories that in its final result machinery is favourable to the workers in capitalist production, because in the change-over from one type of employment to another the newer type is almost invariably an absolute impossibility for the adult worker. This was just as Marx concluded in his long chapter on 'Machinery and Modern Industry': the original victims, whose jobs disappeared with technological change, for the most part starve and perish (CW 3.443; CAP 1.415).

At the end of the 'Outlines' Engels indicated his intention to move on from the effects of machinery to an exposition in detail of the 'despicable immorality' of the factory system (CW 3.443). He did this in *The Condition of the Working Class in England*, researched in 1844 and published in 1845. He referred to that work in 1888 when he wrote, 'How far I had independently progressed towards [Marx's premises] is best shown by my *Condition of the Working Class in England* (SW 1.29). Marx commented in 1859 that Engels 'had by another road (compare his *The Condition of the Working Class in England* in 1844) arrived at the same result as I' (SW 182). The book is Engels's masterpiece, and in undertaking the work there is no doubt that he was proceeding along another road from Marx's critical path through contemporary social theory. The empirical study of working-class life may indeed display Marx's premises as Engels understood them, but the omission of the more theoretical 'Outlines' from Engels's own history of the period (whereas Marx included it) seems obscurely modest, given the use Marx made of his material and the striking way in which Engels anticipated the presuppositions fundamental to Marx's 'new' materialism – living men, their productive activities, and the material world in which these activities take place (CW 5.531).

For Marx the other road taken by Engels proved to be of considerable methodological significance. Curiously it was not a road on which Engels ever travelled again to any significant extent. He surveyed contemporary working-class conditions in England 'from personal observation and authentic sources', as the title-page boldly proclaimed (CW 4.295, 299). For Marx this work represented an introduction to the world of Parliamentary inquiries into poor-relief, factory conditions and child labour; pioneering journalism in radical English newspapers; and other contemporary surveys of proletarian life. This was a world quite separate from the works of economic theory in which he had been immersed, though the connection between the two is obvious. Engels and Marx were both convinced of a discrepancy between the generalisations and prescriptions of the political economists and the real world of capitalist production. This was best documented in Britain, which was not only industrially more advanced than other countries but also freer in allowing and even sponsoring governmental and private inquiries. Engels had material for his book with him when he met with Marx once again in August/September 1844 and their collaboration began. He wrote his manuscript while in Germany, and finished it in March 1845. Publication came in May 1845, a month or so after Engels had joined Marx in Brussels, following the expulsion of communists from Paris in January. Not long after the publication of *The Condition of the Working Class in England* Engels took Marx to Manchester to see it all for himself.

The Condition of the Working Class in England and volume one of *Capital* have a number of common sources, including documents from the Inquiry Commission on the Employment of Children in Factories, the reports of HM Inspectors of Factories, Hansard, and periodicals both radical and establishment. Marx, of course, had many more sources available to him in the 1860s than had Engels in 1844, but apart from that difference the methodology employed and the points made are very much the same. Engels's published work itself served Marx as an important source on which to build his own account, and he enthusiastically recommended it to his readers in a note to *Capital* as an account of conditions up to 1845. Engels's book was referred to ten times by Marx in volume one of *Capital*, with a number of endorsements not merely of its historical relevance but of its actual contents, since in certain branches of industry, so Marx concluded from up-to-date sources, conditions had not changed in the twenty years between the two books:

How completely Engels understood the nature of the capitalist mode of production is shown by the Factory Reports, Reports on Mines, etc., that have appeared since 1845, and how wonderfully he painted the circumstances in detail is seen on the most superficial comparison of his work with the official reports of the Children's Employment Commission, published 18 to 20 years later (1863–1867). These deal especially with the branches of industry in which the Factory Acts had not, up to 1862, been introduced, in fact are not yet introduced. Here, then, little or no alteration had been enforced, by authority, in the conditions painted by Engels (CAP 1.230 n. 2).

In his book Engels surveyed conditions of work before the industrial revolution, the emergence of the industrial and agricultural proletariat (in various trades), the growth of towns to contain the new industrial workers, the effects of competition on proletarians (particularly in times of crisis), immigration, and then a catalogue of specific abuses: physical and moral degradation at work, the horrors of pauperism, and the usurpation by employers of new and exceptional powers over the lives of other human beings. Marx referred most often to Engels's accounts of specific abuses, particularly those that still recurred even when continuously complained of (somewhat hypocritically, according to Marx) in the press.

Marx also used Engels's work in his account of the general process in which manufacture replaced hand-work in industry, most notably in the textile trade. From that Marx drew additional support, so he thought, for the specific theories which he developed in his own economic work, begun in earnest after his reading of Engels's 'Outlines' and *Condition of the Working Class in England* and then summarised in the propositions on the commodity, value and labour which eventually appeared in volume one of *Capital*. Engels's economic theorising never ascended to the level of abstraction reached by Marx; his advice on those sections of *Capital* was concerned exclusively with the presentation of this admittedly difficult material. In that theoretical work Marx had moved on from the major categories of the 'Outlines' – private property and competition – to what Marx himself considered to be the more fundamental phenomenon of value as it operates in industrialised society. Manufacture, according to Marx, 'made it possible for a smaller number of labourers, with the addition of relatively less living labour, not only to consume [e.g.] the wool productively, and put into it new value, but to preserve in the form of yarn etc. its old value'. In this way Marx thought that he had identified, as Smith, Ricardo and the French economist J.-B. Say had not, the specific mechanisms by which the introduction of manufacture in an industry then 'stimulated increased reproduction of [e.g.] wool'. Engels had chronicled just this process for the late eighteenth century, and Marx found this empirical economic history useful in backing up his theoretical claim that 'the constant appropriation of surplus-labour by the capitalists' appears as 'a constant self-expansion of capital' (CAP 568–9).

Most strikingly Marx quoted Engels in support of a political conclusion in *Capital* about the nature of the factory system itself in capitalist society. Marx portrayed the factory owner as a private legislator exercising an autocracy over his workpeople that was quite at odds with the political forms promoted by the bourgeoisie in other spheres: division of responsibility and representation in government. Out of modern mechanised production capitalists had evolved a system of social regulation in which 'the place of the slave driver's lash is taken by the overlooker's book of penalties'. Ironically Marx concluded that violation of the factory-owner's rules was 'if possible, more profitable to him than the keeping of them', and produced detail from Engels, who had declared twenty years earlier that in the 'slavery' binding proletariat to bourgeoisie 'all freedom comes to an end, both at law and in fact' (CAP 1.400 and n.2).

However cold Marx was in November 1842 to the Berlin 'Free' and their associate Friedrich Engels, his political interest in communist-inspired reports from England was demonstrated when Engels's articles continued to appear in *Rheinische Zeitung* under his editorship. That Engels was warmly received in Paris in August 1844 cannot then be attributed to a purely intellectual break with the Berlin Young Hegelians, though this had certainly occurred. Engels's practical activities in England put him in quite another class; most interestingly for Marx those activities were not exclusively political journalism and industrial investigations but included a theoretical project – the 'Outlines of a Critique of Political Economy' – which displayed a knowledge of the literature and an analytical expertise well beyond Marx's current accomplishments. It was that aspect of Engels's work which Marx found most promising in a colleague and collaborator, even though there were no plans at this time or later for joint theoretical work in the economic field. The move from contemporary philosophy and politics towards political economy as the supreme object of critical study was the decisive intellectual test of a colleague for Marx, since his plans for his work from 1844 onwards took a critical account of political economy to be the foundation for whatever other works – on the 'state, law, morals, bourgeois life etc', were envisaged (see Carver (1975), 13 and *passim*).

Engels seems to have surrendered political economy wholly to Marx after 1844 and never to have expressed regret or further independent interest; Marx seems to have taken on this theoretical burden with the driving monomania necessary for a forty-year project and occasionally to have sought Engels's advice on minor points. The work on which they agreed initially to collaborate was one that used Engels's undoubted gifts as a polemicist, satirist and Hegelian insider to best effect. This was a critical attack on their former associates and on Young Hegelian philosophising in general entitled *The Holy Family or Critique of Critical Criticism. Against Bruno Bauer and Company.*

As Marx had explained in early 1844 (in his 'Critique of Hegel's Philosophy of Right. Introduction'), his political project was initially conceived as a definitive critique of German intellectual radicalism, which he considered to be unsound and unserious, by means of the critical destruction of their inspiration, Hegel himself, in the *Philosophy of Right*. In his criticism of this work, so Marx tells us in the preface to the 1844 manuscripts, he recognised the need to disentangle the material on political economy (which he had come to see as fundamental to an understanding of contemporary political and social life) from his critical views on the state, law, morals, etc. and on the Hegelian presuppositions themselves, even as interpreted by readers of Strauss and Feuerbach who rejected any glibly conservative account of Hegel's work. Marx evidently felt the destruction of Young Hegelianism to be imminently necessary, because of its discouraging *political* effect on what he considered to be a real engagement with current issues. That political task was evidently conceived as one that would be swiftly accomplished, leaving him free to pursue his theoretical inquiry into the anatomy of bourgeois society as laid bare by a thorough-going critique of political economy (see Carver (1982), *passim*). The anti-young Hegelian *Holy Family* was planned along the lines of the *Deutsch-Französische Jahrbücher* (which had individually signed contributions), rather than on the model of a large work jointly written. At publication Engels's name appeared before Marx's on the title page. capitalising on his national reputation in Germany, his now declared opposition to former associates, and perhaps even his international connections with other periodicals. By comparison Marx, though an experienced editor, was somewhat obscure (see Carver (1981). chs 1–4).

The effect of Engels's work in the 'Outlines of a Critique of

Political Economy' and *The Condition of the Working Class in England* on Marx, while fully acknowledged, has been hitherto unexplored. The reproduction of theoretical material in *Capital*, similar projections of economic and political trends, an identity of views on certain aspects of communist society, and most intriguingly the very kernel of Marx's premises themselves can all be traced in a detailed comparison of Engels's early work with Marx's critique of political economy from the *Economic and Philosophical Manuscripts* of 1844 to *Capital*. Yet there is little chance that Engels was imparting to Marx thoughts that he was unlikely ever to have had by himself. However strikingly Engels anticipated Marx at this period, there is a clear drift in the latter's work towards the views that Engels expressed. At his most influential Engels represented a short-cut in Marx's development, a considerable inspiration to further efforts and a useful source of supportive material on the history and operation of capitalist industry.

The effect of Marx's thoughts on Engels, or rather of Marx's work as Engels perceived it, was quite different, in that Engels responded by largely abandoning his own empirical researches. A solitary postscript of 1845 to his *Condition of the Working Class in England* was never followed up. Similarly his theoretical work on political economy, in so far as that interest was directed towards serious, independent projects, was suddenly dropped. This response by Engels to the Marx–Engels collaboration was almost the inverse of Marx's, since Marx's theoretical and empirical work grew increasingly to rule his life, at least when the essentials of life itself were not absolutely at the forefront of his concerns. Thus began the famous partnership which flowered with the joint works of the 1840s in which Marx and Engels developed what they called 'our outlook'.

3 'Our Outlook'

Marx and Engels agreed to work together in August 1844; this is attested by their continuing collaboration from that date and by their subsequent memoirs. It is also evident from their initial joint efforts that they aimed to distinguish themselves very sharply from their former associates, with whom they might otherwise continue to be bracketed by present and future sympathisers with the communist cause. Their way of doing this was much more theoretical than political, in an organisational sense, since formal communist organisation hardly existed as yet. Marx and Engels had been in touch with the largely émigré League of the Just in London and Paris, but both evidently declined to join, sensing a lack of analytical discrimination in its members which both men craved (though perhaps to a different extent) in their associates. Thus Marx and Engels set out to distinguish themselves from the theoretically sophisticated and unsophisticated alike, choosing the Young Hegelians as a first and in a sense easier target, since they had more or less organised views to knock down.

Marx's early journalism showed him to be a dialectician in the classical manner: he established his arguments, in the first instance, through successive refutations of plausible but ultimately unsatisfactory theses selected to serve the author's didactic purposes. Engels employed this method to some extent in his 'Outlines of Political Economy', though he was rather less diffident than the critically scrupulous Marx in setting out his own positive views. *A Critique of Critical Criticism. Against Bruno Bauer and Co.* by Friedrich Engels and Karl Marx was given the further appellation *The Holy Family* on the suggestion of the publisher, who thus summarised the authors' extended metaphor that the Young Hegelians were at bottom idealist philosophers and possibly crypto-Christians devoted to a pure realm of ideas beyond mundane reality. Engels completed his portion of the work very quickly and left Paris in September 1844 for Barmen; Marx laboured until November, expanding the work quite beyond their original expectations.

At the opening of the book Engels and Marx identified Bruno Bauer and the contributors to his *Allgemeine Literatur-Zeitung* as adherents of '*speculative idealism*', which they declared to be 'in all respects *below* the level already attained by German theoretical development'. Evidently this made its demolition all the more urgent; it was to be accomplished by asserting 'the already achieved results' by contrast. Further development was put forward to 'the independent works in which we – each of us for himself, of course – shall present our positive view' (CW 4.7–8). Other than the jointly-written *German Ideology* and Communist Manifesto, and a number of short communications and articles, jointly signed, Marx and Engels stuck to this programme of independent publication throughout the rest of their careers. Such exchanges of information as occurred are wholly insufficient to support a general theory of joint authorship (notwithstanding the appearance of only one name on the various title-pages), nor does the extensive manuscript material which is preserved lead to the conclusion that the two thought as one. A theory that joint authorship occurred in unrecorded conferences does not square with the recorded comments of the two men, since these do not suggest that intensive collaboration had already taken place. Their queries and replies frankly tended towards the superficial even when important published works of the two authors were mentioned.

Engels wrote the opening sections of *The Holy Family*, criticising 'Bauer and Co.' primarily for factual errors in their comments on British politics, industrial development, technology and the manufacturing process itself. He ridiculed their high-flown consideration of social issues and concluded: 'Formulae, nothing but formulae.' These were merely constructed, he wrote, 'out of the existing *Hegelian* philosophy and the existing social aspirations' (CW 4.20). Engels satirised a rather pompously self-conscious philosophy by portraying it as Hegel's God-like Spirit, loving in its consciousness but irremediably abstract. The link here with his previous theological satires is unmistakable, as is the re-use of material from his 'Condition of England' articles published earlier in 1844 while he was collecting material for his empirical study of the English working class.

Marx's criticisms were more fundamental, though perhaps less academically justifiable in that they relied on the demolition of a common philosophical position imputed to 'Critical Criticism', which he took to be a simple-minded use of the subject – predicate reversal that Feuerbach had recommended in making sense of Hegel: 'By this simple process, by changing the predicate into the subject, all the attributes and manifestations of human nature can be Critically transformed ... Thus, for example, Critical Criticism makes criticism, as a predicate and activity of man, into a subject apart' (CW 4.21).

However, Marx spent little time on what he later described with amusement as 'the cult of Feuerbach' (see McLellan (1973), 135 n. 2), but directed his criticism of the 'critical critics' to *their* treatment of P.-J. Proudhon's widely read *What Is Property?*, first published in 1840 with a second edition in 1841. Self-consciously building on Engels's 'Outlines', Marx advanced his own work on political economy ('our main interest') by defending Proudhon, while also declaring his work to be somewhat inferior to the much less publicised 'Outlines' in the *Deutsch-Französische Jahrbücher*. Proudhon used 'economic premises' when he argued against the political economists, whereas Engels considered what *appeared* to be premises – the categories wages, trade, value, price, money etc. – as 'forms of private property in themselves'. By claiming a connection between these surface phenomena and one underlying category, Engels's work was analytically more elegant and potentially much more powerful. Even so, Proudhon's critical investigation was 'the first resolute, ruthless, and at the same time scientific investigation' of the 'the basis of political economy, *private property*', and Marx had had his eye on it for some time, describing it in an article of October 1842 as 'sharp-witted' (CW 4.31–4; CW 1.220). Engels had praised

Proudhon's work extravagantly in *The New Moral World* in November 1843, and this perhaps reinforced Marx's ever-critical enthusiasm for an appreciative confrontation:

> This is the most philosophical work, on the part of the Communists, in the French language; and, if I wish to see any French book translated into the English language, it is this. The right of private property, the consequences of this institution, competition, immorality, misery, are here developed with a power of intellect, and real scientific research, which I never since found united in a single volume (CW 3.399).

After establishing a critical hierarchy in contemporary comment on political economy – Engels, Proudhon, the 'critical critics' in that descending order – Marx struck out on his own, using material freshly written in the *Economic and Philosophical Manuscripts* of 1844. The methodology, however, was adapted from Engels's 'Outlines', where there was a focus on 'contradictions' in social life:

> ... political economy operates in permanent contradiction to its basic premise, private property ... The economists themselves occasionally feel these contradictions ... Thus, as an exception ... the economists occasionally stress the semblance of humanity in economic relations, but sometimes, and as a rule, they take these relations precisely in their clearly pronounced *difference* from the human (CW 4.32–3).

Proudhon, like Engels, took 'the *human semblance* of the economic relations seriously' and contrasted to it the '*inhuman reality*' of real conditions. Like Engels, he found the root of all economic contradiction in private property as such and in its entirety, rather than in its specific forms such as wages, profit, etc. The '*essence of private property*', Marx concluded, was 'the vital question of political economy and jurisprudence', *the* point on which communists must be crystal clear. The 'critical critics' missed this utterly and spread confusion in their works through a faulty, superficial methodology remote from what Marx termed the 'real movement' which he aimed to clarify (CW 4.33, 35).

Proudhon had proceeded from 'the poverty bred by the movement of private property', sophistically concealed, Marx claimed, by political economy, but central to the concerns of communists (Engels's *Condition of the Working Class in England* was, as Marx knew, then in preparation). Political economy had proceeded from wealth 'which the movement of private property [in production and trade], supposedly creates for the *nations*'. 'Proletariat and wealth are opposites', Marx declared, but 'the question is exactly what place each occupies in the antithesis'. Critical criticism, he wrote, had merely declared them to be two sides of a single whole and thereby remained *outside* the object with which it pretended to deal (CW 4.34–5).

The 'real movement' of private property was depicted by Marx in stark contrast to the 'speculative antitheses' of critical criticism. Although proletariat and private property as wealth were antithetical, the positive and negative sides of this antithesis were, for Marx, real, specifiable processes in society: 'since the conditions of life of the proletariat sum up all the conditions of life of society today in their most inhuman form; since man... is driven directly to revolt against this inhumanity, it follows that the proletariat can and must emancipate itself'. 'A large part of the English and French proletariat is already *conscious* of its historic task', Marx wrote, 'and is constantly working to develop that consciousness into complete clarity' (CW 4.36–7).

Marx's critical treatment of political economy was to be his contribution to this international movement, and there is little doubt that in a theoretical sense he regarded this task as the decisive step towards 'clarity' (CW 4.37). How precisely Marx's severe notions of theoretical exactitude were to make their impact on proletarian politics in a practical sense was presumably to be worked out as communists and proletarians joined together, an activity which Marx and Engels supported during this period, most notably in Brussels where they moved in 1845. Proudhon himself was accurately declared by Marx to have been 'a proletarian, an *ouvrier*', and his work was 'a scientific manifesto of the French proletariat' – as opposed to the 'literary botch work' of the critical critics. Yet Proudhon, as stated earlier, remained captive to the premises of political economy in his category '*possession*', which was not appropriately developed (CW 4.41–3).

Similarly Proudhon's treatment of the labour theory of

value was on the right track, but still within economic premises of the sort Marx aimed to expose: 'By making labour time ... the measure of wages and the determinant of the value of the product, Proudhon makes the human side the decisive factor. In old political economy, on the other hand, the decisive factor was the material power of capital and of landed property'. 'In other words', Marx concluded, 'Proudhon reinstates man in his rights, but still in an economic and therefore contradictory way' (CW 4.49).

Marx's real contrast to the critical critics as 'absolute idealists' was not Proudhon, despite the merits of his 'scientific manifesto', nor Engels, whose superior analytical grip on political economy was highly praised, but contemporary workers themselves when they 'formed associations in which they exchange opinions not only on their immediate needs as *workers*, but on their needs as *human beings*'. Thus Marx's work was not intended to be merely another point of view derived from pure intellectual speculation but was rather to take its presuppositions and subject-matter from life as experienced in the Manchester or Lyons workshops. There 'property, capital, money, wage-labour and the like are no ideal figments of the brain but very practical, very objective products' that, according to Marx, 'must be abolished in a practical, objective way, for man to become man' (CW 4.52–3). However obvious and inevitable Marx considered this movement to be, it was sharply distinguished (in his mind, anyway) from teleological, and particularly Hegelian philosophies of history, to which philosophers and pseudo-philosophers appealed in support of their general views on man, his fate and the meaning of life. Marx would have none of it:

For Herr [Bruno] Bauer, as for Hegel, truth is an *automaton* that proves itself. Man must *follow* it ... Just as, according to the earlier teleologists, plants exist to be eaten by animals, and animals to be eaten by men, history exists in order to serve as the act of consumption of theoretical eating – *proving*. Man exists so that history may exist, and history exists ... so that *truth* may arrive at *self-consciousness* ... This is why Absolute Criticism uses phrases like these: '*History* does not allow itself to be mocked ... [etc.]' (CW 4.79).

Moreover, in Marx's view, '*History* does *nothing*', it

'"possesses *no* immense wealth"', it '"wages *no* battles"'. It is 'real, living man who does all that, who possesses and fights . . . history is *nothing but* the activity of man pursuing his aims' (CW 4.93). Marx's historical judgements were derived, so he claimed, from consideration of 'empirical man' who lives 'deep down in an English cellar or at the top of a French block of flats'; these judgements were not derived from 'history' as 'an ethereal subject' (CW 4.80).

Empirical man had been considered by communist and socialist writers with some degree of accuracy, despite various flaws in their understanding of economic life and, often, an oversimplified view of the difficulties involved in rectifying the horrors wrought by modern society. Still, 'the communist criticism', Marx wrote, 'had practically at once as its counterpart the movement of the *great mass*... One must know the studiousness, the craving for knowledge, the moral energy and the unceasing urge for development of the French and English workers to be able to form an idea of the *human* nobility of this movement' (CW 4.84). In considering socialism, 'critical criticism' had missed this altogether and would never get near it, because of a dilettante approach, a lack of resolution in seeking what Marx called '*a* social theory', and an overall purposelessness in theorising:

Criticism is talking here about *Fourierism* – if it is talking about anything – and in particular of the Fourierism of *La Démocratie pacifique* [newspaper published 1843–51 in Paris]. But this is far from being the 'social theory' of the French. The French have *social theories*, but not *a* social theory; the diluted Fourierism that *La Démocratie pacifique* preaches is nothing but the social doctrine of a section of the philanthropic bourgeoisie. The people is *communistic*, and, as a matter of fact, split into a multitude of different groups; the true movement and the elaboration of these different social shades is not only not *exhausted*, it is really only *beginning*. But it will not end in pure, i.e., abstract, *theory* as Critical Criticism would like it to; it will end in a quite *practical practice* that will not bother at all about the categorical categories of Criticism (CW 4.152–3).

Marx's alternative was the unity of theory and practice, modelled on a pre-existing unity in real life, pointing particularly to England (as described by Engels) and to France, as he experienced it himself. This was, of course, a highly selective account of experience, but for Marx the trend towards a unity of revolutionary theory and proletarian practice was potentially of much more significance than other aspects of life, working-class or otherwise:

The criticism of the French and the English is not an abstract, preternatural personality outside mankind; it is the *real human activity* of individuals who are active members of society and who suffer, feel, think and act as human beings. That is why their criticism is at the same time practical, their communism a socialism in which they give practical, concrete measures, and in which they not only think but even more act, it is the living, real criticism of existing society, the recognition of the causes of 'the decay' (CW 4.153).

To aid this practical activity Marx proposed a theoretical project, the elements of which were present in 'Critical Criticism' but in the wrong relationship:

Its own [Critical Criticism's] theory is confined to stating that everything determinate is an opposite of the boundless generality of self-consciousness and is, therefore, of no significance; for example, the state, private property, etc. It must be shown, on the contrary, how the state, private property, etc., turn human beings into abstractions, or are products of *abstract* man, instead of being the reality of individual, concrete human beings (CW 4.193).

Engels's work in *The Holy Family* showed him to be a skilful polemicist in exposing factual error and Hegelian mumbo-jumbo. His view of the progressive character of certain developments in working-class politics, particularly Chartism, and his rejection of philosophical idealism were both in evidence. For Young Hegelian error he put forward fact and for their idealism he substituted an implicit realism in which, as he put it about a year earlier in the 'Outlines', production takes place, involving men, 'active physically and mentally', and nature (CW 3.428). Evidently the more explicit theoretical treatment of the alternative to Young Hegelian idealism was left to Marx who stated that, contrary to the predilections of the critical critics, 'there is a world in which *consciousness* and *being* are distinct; a world which continues to exist when I merely abolish its existence in thought ... i.e., when I modify my own subjective consciousness without altering the objective reality in a really objective way'. To the critical critics' 'world of *self-consciousness*' Marx opposed 'my own *objective* reality and that of other men' (CW 4.192–3). 'Objective reality' for Marx was 'industry... the immediate mode of production of life itself', which proceeds from 'the theoretical and practical relation of man to nature, i.e. natural science and industry', the very premises put forward by Engels when he discussed production in his 'Outlines' (CW 4.150).

This was the world of Marx's 'opposites'—proletariat and wealth. These were opposites, because wealth was private property and the proletariat, through the competitive system of production, could get little of it. The key to this world, so Marx revealed, lay in political economy. The difficulty for communists was that political economy itself presupposed and justified private property; hence its presuppositions and apologetic aspects must be overcome by thorough criticism. Engels had begun this task, but judging from Marx's work on Proudhon, and his particular focus on the labour theory of value (treated only cursorily by Engels), it was Marx who proposed to finish the job. On 1 February 1845, just after seeing *The Holy Family* through the press, Marx signed a contract for a *Critique of Politics and Political Economy* (see Carver (1975), 12–14).

While Marx's work was acquiring a certain kind of theoretical momentum in terms of clarity of subject matter, purpose and presuppositions, Engels continued in his role as publicist, propagandist and reporter for the communist cause, writing for both German and English audiences and giving, *inter alia*, published notice of 'Messrs Marx and Engels... detailed refutation [in *The Holy Family*] of the principles advocated by B. Bauer'; 'Dr Marx's forthcoming *Review of Politics and Political and Political Economy*'; and 'Mr F. Engels' *Condition of the Working Classes of Great Britain*' (CW 4.240–1). In one of his articles, disbelieving Germans were given an account of 'Recently Founded Communist Colonies still in Existence' to counter objections that communism – 'social existence and activity based on community of goods' – was inherently impractical with respect to menial and unpleasant tasks and to the equal claim by all on communal possessions.

Engels disposed of the first line of objection by citing community spirit and improved technology, and of the second by commenting that 'all communist colonies so far have become so enormously rich after ten or fifteen years that they have everything they can desire in greater abundance than they can consume, so that no grounds for dispute exist'. Engels's source was mainly a series of letters published in the radical English press covering American colonies – Shakers, Harmonists, Separatists – and the English Owenites, though Engels distanced communism as such from the religious practices of these communities. 'Of the more recent colonies', he commented, 'almost all are in any case quite free of religious nonsense' (CW 214–15). The conclusions Engels drew for his German readers prefigured the directness of the Communist Manifesto and its thesis that part of the bourgeoisie would join the proletariat:

If the workers are united among themselves, hold together and pursue *one* purpose, they are infinitely stronger than the rich. And if, moreover, they have set their sights upon such a rational purpose, and one which desires the best for all mankind, as community of goods, it is self-evident that the better and more intelligent among the rich will declare themselves in agreement with the workers and support them (CW 4.227–8).

For the English audience Engels reviewed the 'Rapid Progress of Communism in Germany', writing that socialism had progressed miraculously there over the preceding two years and chronicling the 'first Socialist publication... a year ago [the *Deutsch-Französische Jahrbücher*]'. Though there were 'some hundreds of German Communists' abroad, legal restrictions and official discouragement at home limited their influence. Engels's definition of socialism encompassed all societies 'for ameliorating the condition of the working people', so his claim that 'a strong Socialist party has grown up' is not quite so astonishing as it appears. Admitting that the stronghold of socialism is the middle class, Engels noted that 'we, however, hope to be in a short time supported by the working classes, who always, and everywhere, must form the strength and body of the Socialist party', thus introducing the communist perspective without the immediate *frisson* atten-

dant on the name. Anyway, Engels informed his readers that
the German middle class 'is far more disinterested, impartial,
and intelligent, than in England', though this was because it
was poorer. Excitedly Engels looked forward to a community
erected by 'practical men of business', building on the experiences of Owen, Fourier, American communities, and
English experiments; the 'most active literary characters' in
German Socialism were listed separately and included Marx,
Engels and Hess (CW 4.229–32).

Engels's next instalment on 'Rapid Progress' was much
more straightforward about *communism* and its principles –
'organisation of labour, protection of labour against the
power of capital, etc.' (CW 4.234–6). And in the final
article he summarised various communist speeches, recently
delivered, among them his own at Elberfeld, in which
'Mr Engels...proved...that the present state of Germany
was such as could not but produce in a very short time a social
revolution'. Moreover, 'this imminent revolution was not to be
averted by any possible measures for promoting commerce and
manufacturing industry' but could only be prevented by the
'introduction of, and the preparation for, the Community
system'. Otherwise there would be 'a revolution more terrible
than any of the mere subversions of past history'
(CW 4.238–9).

These meetings in Elberfeld mobilised middle-class opinion,
according to Engels, because 'nearly every patrician and
moneyed family of the town had one of its members [e.g.
Friedrich Engels] or relatives present at the large table
occupied by the Communists'. In conclusion he virtually wrote
off socialism in favour of communism; this was perhaps a
matter of tactics in *gradually* introducing an English socialist
audience to a more radical, revolutionary and class-conscious
perspective. In Germany, he wrote, 'the word Socialism means
nothing but the different vague, undefined, and undefinable
imaginations of those who see that something must be done,
and who yet cannot make up their minds to go the whole length
of the Community system' (CW 4.239–41).

The 'Speeches in Elberfeld' to which Engels referred were
delivered on 8 and 15 February 1845 and published in August.
There is nothing like them in Marx's works to that date, partly

no doubt because Marx lacked the opportunity to address an influential non-academic audience in public, but partly because his style – learned, complex, ultra-intellectual – was more suited to a semi-censored paper than to middle-class meetings. Marx's later attempts (in Brussels and London) to present his work in a simple, oral style were directed at working-class audiences and were confined to the basic elements of his economic criticism. Engels was obviously at home with the middle classes of Elberfeld, and his presentation – factual, graphic, oriented to business and politics – must have struck the right level, even if one discounts Engels's own version of his success:

...not a word was offered in reply...a few days afterwards those who had publicly advocated our cause were overrun by numbers of people who asked for books and papers from which they might get a view of the whole system (CW 4.238, 240).

The 'Speeches' presented aspects of Engels's rather more complex 'Outlines' in simple, discursive terms that one recognises now as the familiar cadences of the Communist Manifesto. Free competition was the basic economic assumption from which he drew his communist conclusion: 'Thus there arises the glaring contradiction between a few rich people on the one hand, and many poor on the other... the contradiction will develop more and more sharply until finally necessity compels society to reorganise itself on more rational principles' (CW 4.244).

Free competition was irrational, Engels wrote, because 'each man works on his own, each strives for his own enrichment and is not in the least concerned with what the rest are doing'. 'All of us work each for his own advantage, unconcerned about the welfare of others', whereas 'it is an obvious, self-evident truth that the interest, the well-being, the happiness of every individual is inseparably bound up with that of his fellow-men'. As long as bourgeois society remains a 'war of all against all' this unregulated economic system will lead to disaster, in particular to the ruin of the small middle class, who were presumably numerous in Engels's audience and doubtless terrified of the propertyless fate he foresaw for them (CW 243–8). Engels wrote excitedly to Marx (on 22

February – 7 March 1845) that 'All Elberfeld and Barmen were there, from money-aristocracy to grocery, excepting only the proletariat'. He estimated attendance at the three meetings as successively 40, 130 and 200 (MEGA (New Series) III/1.267).

A system predicated on opposed interests in free competition led, in Engels's view, to 'a crying disproportion between production and consumption' and the terrors of commercial crisis. Manufacturers work haphazardly, relying on the constantly fluctuating level of prices which inevitably leads to interruptions in trade, short-time working, bankruptcies, stock clearance and the loss of capital. Communism would solve these difficulties:

> In communist society, where the interests of individuals are not opposed to one another but, on the contrary, are united, competition is eliminated... In communist society it will be easy to be informed about both production and consumption. Since we know how much, on the average, a person needs, it is easy to calculate how much is needed by a given number of individuals, and since production is no longer in the hands of private producers but in those of the community and its administrative bodies, it is a trifling matter *to regulate production according to needs* (CW 4.243–6).

Other evils which would be abolished in communist society included 'intermediary swindlers, speculators, agents, exporters, commission agents' etc. (all anathema to small manufacturers), crimes against property (which would 'cease of their own accord where everyone receives what he needs to satisfy his natural and spiritual urges'), standing armies (since revolution and aggressive war would be unthinkable, though national defence would be willingly undertaken), waste of 'labour power' in useless domestic service, unemployment and prostitution. One further result would be a reduction of 'present customary labour time' by half, since waste and disadvantageous use of labour would be eliminated (CW 4.246–52).

All this was not mere theory, Engels claimed, because it was not 'rooted in pure fantasy' but took reality into account. The English, he opined, 'will probably begin by setting up a number of colonies and leaving it to every individual whether to join or not', whereas the French 'will be likely to prepare and implement communism on a national basis'. By way of German preparation Engels suggested universal state education, reorganisation of poor relief so that the destitute would work for themselves in colonies rather than for private employers, and the introduction of progressive taxation on capital to finance those measures. Thus common ownership would not be introduced 'overnight and against the will of the nation' (CW 4.253–5).

In his next speech Engels returned to the possibility of social revolution, giving his three measures towards 'practical communism' greater bite:

The proletariat must under all circumstances not only continue to exist but also enlarge itself continually, become an ever more threatening power in our society as long as we continue to produce each on his own and in opposition to everyone else. But one day the proletariat will attain a level of power and of insight at which it will no longer tolerate the pressure of the entire social structure always bearing down on its shoulders, when it will demand a more even distribution of social burdens and rights; and then – unless human nature has changed by that time – a social revolution will be inevitable (CW 4.253, 257).

Neither free-trade nor protectionism would save German industry, he argued: 'proceeding from competition in general... the unavoidable result of our existing social relations... will be a *social revolution*'. That revolution, he deduced, would be 'far fiercer and bloodier than all those that preceded it' and will moreover not stop half-way but 'will deal with the real causes of want and poverty, of ignorance and crime... by the proclamation of the principles of communism'. This deduction was based on two claims: 1) that previous revolutions in England and France had realised what they aimed for, and 2) that the contemporary labour movements in those countries were '*all* based on the principle of common property', excepting only the adherents of Fourier. To his audience Engels recommended the 'peaceful introduction or at least preparation of communism' to avoid 'the *bloody* solution of the social problem'. In conclusion he portrayed communism as a generalisation of some of the things members of the middle-class audience undoubtedly wanted for themselves: 'no need to fear any violent shattering of [one's] condition', and more provocatively a release from 'the semblance' of enjoyment they might have in their present station within a deeply contradictory and disordered society (CW 4.261–4).

Engels promoted communism in an analysis that seemed complete, and it operated in terms familiar to his middle-class readers and audiences. He took free competition as his framework, deduced the necessity of crises, proletarianisation and unemployment, and produced a plausible account of a future in which working-class consciousness coincided with more theoretical speculation on man and society. Even 'Dr Feuerbach, the most eminent philosophical genius in Germany at the present time, has declared himself a Communist', Engels wrote in *The New Moral World*. According to his unidentified informant, Feuerbach viewed communism as a necessary consequence of the principle he had formulated, and that Communism was, in fact, only 'The *practice* of what he had proclaimed long before theoretically'. Now he felt 'much inclined' to dedicate his next work to Wilhelm Weitling, the working-class communist. 'Dr Marx', said Engels, had predicted this 'union between the German philosophers...and the German working men' in the *Deutsch-Französische Jahrbücher*, where he wrote that the '*head* of this emancipation [of man] is *philosophy*, its *heart* is the *proletariat*' (CW 3.187; CW 4.235–6).

None of Marx's writings for this period shows the sweep that Engels displayed in his analysis, which reappears in the jointly written Communist Manifesto and in disjointed fashion in Marx's *Capital* itself. At the time, however, that Engels promulgated communism as a deductive exercise from political economy, provided that free competition was correctly understood, Marx was digging beneath that category to private property (Engels's 'opposed interests') and deeper still to the concept of value itself. However rudimentary his work at this stage, and however far removed from the later sophistication of *Capital*, there is still a discernible *direction* of inquiry in Marx's work that is lacking, for whatever reason, contingent or intellectual, in Engels's more polished and influential efforts up to the spring of 1845.

While Marx pursued his economic researches, now using English texts as well as French, Engels was starting, so he said in a letter to Marx of 20 January 1845, a work on English history and socialism. While we have no manuscript material, it seems reasonable to assume this to be the 'more comprehensive work on the social history of England' mentioned in the preface to *The Condition of the Working Class in England* and a continuation of his works of 1843–4 for e.g., the *Deutsch-Französische Jahrbücher* and *Vorwärts*, the Paris paper with which Marx and Engels were associated during their stay there. Engels had actually completed a long review of Thomas Carlyle's *Past and Present* entitled 'The Condition of England' and two further articles on 'The Eighteenth Century' and 'The English Constitution' in 1844 (MEGA (New Series) III/1.260; CW 4.302). Thus in the early months of their partnership Engels brought to Marx works of exciting sophistication in two fields: economic criticism (the 'Outlines of a Critique of Political Economy'), and contemporary empirical research and observation (*The Condition of the Working Class in England*). These studies, and a third – the history of the industrial revolution — were of profound interest to Marx. Yet he had done little if any work on two – industrial development and contemporary observation – and had merely begun, with agonising thoroughness, a critical investigation of political economy. Those economic studies were summarised to a certain degree in the *Economic and Philosophical Manuscripts* of mid-1844, but at a high level of substantive and methodological abstraction. Perhaps Marx could have worked his way from that level to the specific consideration of German, even Rhenish social conditions and politics undertaken by Engels in his 'Speeches in Elberfeld', when he moved from his 'Outlines' to contemporary communist politics. Perhaps not, but the obvious utility of Engels's work – on the history, theory and contemporary politics of industrial society – challenges us to consider what, after all, was the real character of Marx's early writings.

From his early journalism onwards, Marx was involved with the 'social question', i.e. the treatment of the poor in contemporary society, yet his tactics – using a liberal paper – meant that his focus had to be on official politics and politicians, whom he criticised with merciless but highly abstract arguments concerning man, citizenship, the law, rights and freedom. German radicals found little favour with Marx, as we have seen, and his weapons against them were similarly devastating yet remote from actual experience. The social world which Marx portrayed, in contrast to a Young Hegelian cloud-land, presented material production as the paradigm for man's real relationship with nature. Alluding to that world, however, was rather different from writing its history, chronicling its depredations and giving a theoretical account of its operation. Engels had done all these – to a minimal but reasonable standard of accuracy, comprehensiveness and analytical elegance. Marx had not.

However, Marx had the wit to recognise that abstract arguments, though ultimately devastating against fairly sophisticated opponents, would not by themselves crush the opposition, whether liberal or idealist or both. The 'social question' and the 'objective world' coincided analytically in *his* mind, but the history and current state of industrial society were essential specifications of this 'outlook' that would reveal its plausibility and political character. The theoretical study of political economy would reveal its truth.

On returning to Brussels from Manchester in late summer 1845, Marx and Engels discovered that 'Bauer and Co.' were not devastated by *The Holy Family* but had dared to reply. Marx and Engels responded anonymously in the same Leipzig periodical: 'By resorting to incompetent *jugglery*, to the most deplorable conjuring trick, *Bruno Bauer* has in the final analysis confirmed the death sentence passed upon him by *Engels* and *Marx* in *The Holy Family*'. (CW 5.18). A mere response, however, was not good enough. Commenting on his career in 1859 Marx wrote that 'in the spring of 1845 ... we resolved to work out in common the opposition of our view to the ideological view of German philosophy, in fact, to settle accounts with our erstwhile philosophical conscience. The resolve was carried out in the form of a criticism of post-Hegelian philosophy' (SW 182–3).

While working on the manuscript (never published as a whole in Marx's or Engels's lifetimes) Marx wrote excuses to the prospective publisher of his *Critique of Politics and Political Economy*: 'It seemed very important to me to *preface* my *positive* work with a polemic against German philosophy and contemporary *German socialism*... to prepare the public for the basis of my economic work which is wholly opposed to previous studies in Germany' (MEGA (New Series) III/2.23). The representatives of modern German philosophy attacked in *The German Ideology* were Ludwig Feuerbach, Bruno Bauer and Max Stirner (author of the recently published *Ego and Its Own*) (CW 5.19). This group was surely the 'erst-while philosophical conscience' mentioned by Marx. In much of the literature on *The German Ideology* it is erroneously assumed that Marx and Engels (see SW 584) were referring to their own 'conscience' as formerly philosophical and thus, it is erroneously concluded, the two were somehow rejecting philosophy as such. While there is no doubt that Marx and Engels rejected ideology, academic philosophy, moralising and nonsense generally, a rejection of philosophy as a whole is virtually meaningless, given the *theoretical* character of Marx's critique of political economy, in which philosophical concepts were openly employed (such as 'quality' and 'quantity' in *Capital*). Late in life Engels involved himself in what he termed 'basic' questions (e.g. mind and matter) which were resolved, so he claimed, according to the 'Marxist world outlook'. While distinct, in Engels's view, from conventional philosophy, the origin of those issues and many of the terms were unmistakably philosophical, and it would be a very precious quibble to maintain that in some sense what Marx and Engels declared in *The German Ideology* was that their work would henceforth dispense with philosophy altogether, when in fact they continued to work hard straightening out philosophers, using philosophy in their works and revising philosophy itself – implicitly (Marx's usual mode), and explicitly (as Engels did in the 1870s and 1880s).

Though Marx and Engels achieved a definitive formulation of their 'view' in *The German Ideology*, the conventional assumption that their earlier works proceeded on some other basis is not warranted. As we have seen, the premises of *The German Ideology* can be traced explicitly in Marx's work to the 1843 'Letters' to the *Deutsch-Französische Jahrbücher* and implicitly in the journalism of 1842, despite the liberal – Young Hegelian context and liberal audience. Engels, never as theoretically focussed as Marx, displayed the premises of *The German Ideology* in his 'Outlines', and we can trace his concern with industrial production back to the 'Letters from Wuppertal' of 1839. However inexplicit were his premises, and however various were his judgements in selecting topics and dispensing praise and criticism, there is a recurrent theme in Engels's works that sets him apart from a vague but simple concern with poverty and revolution and identifies him as peculiarly conscious of the role of productive activities in society and politics.

The German Ideology was a true collaboration by Marx and Engels, in that they seem genuinely to have written it together (though they also solicited some contributions from Moses Hess). The manuscript occupied them from November 1845 to about August 1846; Engels wrote up some further material on 'The True Socialists' (presented in the original manuscript as a philosophical amalgamation of English and French communist ideas) the following year. The authors could not find a publisher, so Marx informed us in 1859, and as a result they 'abandoned the manuscript to the gnawing criticism of the mice'. This was tantalising news for his readers, who might have wondered why they were informed in a short autobiographical sketch about a work they could never expect to obtain. 'Self-clarification' was the main purpose, according to Marx, and the authors advanced together and individually to other projects which 'put our views before the public ... now from one aspect, now from another' (SW 183).

What exactly was clarified, and to whom, in *The German Ideology* is of particular importance, because the work made explicit the premises held by Marx and Engels, and as such we have a prolegomenon to later writings in which this material is presupposed, but not stated in so many words. Moreover Engels revisited this period later in life and provided his own 'short, coherent account of our relation to the Hegelian philosophy' in a far more influential work published after Marx's death (SW 584). Whether he was right about the content of *The German Ideology*, the relation of his and Marx's earlier works to it, and the contributions each author made to the work, can only be judged if *The German Ideology* is scrutinised in its context without the benefit of Engels's later gloss.

The initial section of *The German Ideology* recapitulated, in a sense, much of Marx's and Engels's previous work. Young and Old Hegelians were equated as idealists and their differences dismissed as superficial or misleading. Both 'attribute an independent existence' to 'conceptions, thoughts, ideas... all the products of consciousness'. These they declare to be the bonds or chains of society (Old and Young Hegelians, respectively), and from the Young Hegelian point of view it follows that one need fight 'only against these illusions' to be free. Thus Young Hegelians put to men 'the moral postulate of exchanging their present consciousness for human, critical or egoistic consciousness' (Feuerbach, B. Bauer and Stirner, respectively). In Marx and Engels' view, however, these Young Hegelians were 'in no way combating the real existing world' when they fought phrases with phrases. The conclusion drawn by Marx and Engels pointed to the economic, historical, empirical and even political work undertaken pre-eminently by Engels: 'It has not occurred to any one of these philosophers to inquire into the connection of German philosophy with German reality, the connection of their criticism with their own material surroundings' (CW 5.29–30).

In order to do that, genuinely non-idealist premises were required, and here we detect Marx's sharp analytical mind at work on material dating in explicit form to Engels's 'Outlines', and implicitly to much earlier work by both authors. These premises were defined as 'real' and clearly distinguished from any abstraction that might be made from them: 'They are the real individuals, their activity and the material conditions of their life, both those which they find already existing and those produced by their activity'. Production, the authors continued, distinguishes man from other animals *in practice*, and from this premise they proceeded to characterise production as such and production as it had developed within and (more speculatively) before the historical record. From there it was not difficult to establish a general relationship between 'productive forces, the division of labour and internal intercourse', and a more particular account of the historical development of production (in Europe, though this is unstated). Their conclusion was that the relative position of groups in society (e.g. states, classes) is determined by the way work is organised (CW 5.31–7).

With this established, the authors announced a programme for studying 'the actual life-process and the activity of the individuals of each epoch'. The methodology was to be empirical (no 'empty phrases'), though abstractions derived from observation would play a role in arranging material and indicating sequence. In no way would the abstractions function as 'a self-sufficient philosophy' of the idealist type for 'neatly trimming the epochs of history', including presumably future epochs. Once again the Hegelian-style philosophy of history was rejected; a realm of abstractions to which human life could not but eventually conform was explicitly ruled out (CW 5.37).

Thus Marx and Engels did not reject a role for individuals in historical and contemporary events; their study presupposed individuals whose activities have characteristically resulted in the formation of groups such as estates or classes whose political significance was obvious. It is this explicit linkage between the generalities of the man – Nature relationship and the specifics of the socio-political groups in which communists were interested that makes *The German Ideology* an important collective achievement for Marx and Engels. The historical and empirical material employed to illustrate this scheme was largely derived from Engels's work on England; the vehement and telling anti-idealism was reminiscent of both authors in their previous polemics, though the material was mostly Marx's – there is even use of a section on Democritus and Epicurus from his doctoral dissertation begun in 1839 (CW 5.140–2). The crisp concern with premises was also probably Marx's contribution – the *Theses on Feuerbach* preceded Engels's return to Brussels and the initial work on *The German Ideology* by perhaps a few weeks.

Marx's later account of his 'guiding thread' in his 1859 Preface to *A Contribution to the Critique of Political Economy* reproduced the theoretical material in *The German Ideology* in very similar phrases. An extended comparison between the two texts not only reveals that Marx's initial premises held good in the later summary of his basic view of society and social change; such a comparison also sheds much-needed light on the somewhat murky yet highly influential 1859 propositions themselves, particularly when *The German Ideology* challenges us to re-think traditional interpretations of the 'guiding thread':

The German Ideology (1845–6)	Preface (1859)
Empirical observation must in each separate instance bring out empirically, and without any mystification and speculation, the connection of the social and political structure with production (CW 5.35).	My investigation led to the result that legal relations as well as forms of state are to be grasped neither from themselves nor from the so-called general development of the human mind, but rather have their roots in the material conditions of life (SW 181).
The fact is, therefore, that definite individuals who are productively active in a definite way enter into these definite social and political relations... They work under definite material limits, presuppositions and conditions independent of their will (CW 5.35–6).	In the social production of their life, men enter into definite relations that are indispensable and independent of their will... (SW 181).
...the whole internal structure of the nation itself depends on the stage of development reached by its production and its internal and external intercourse (CW 5.32).	...relations of production which correspond to a definite stage of development of their material productive forces (SW 181).
The social structure and the state are continually evolving out of the life-process of definite individuals... (CW 5.35).	...the economic structure of society, the real foundation, on which rises a legal and political superstructure... (SW 181).
The various stages of development in the division of labour are just so many different forms of property... (CW 5.32).	...existing relations of production, or – what is but a legal expression for the same thing –... property relations (SW 181).
This mode of production must not be considered simply as being the reproduction of the physical existence of the indi-	The mode of production of material life conditions the social, political and intellectual life process in general (SW 181).

viduals. Rather it is a definite form of activity of these individuals, a definite form of expressing their life, a definite *mode of life* on their part. As individuals express their life, so they are. What they are, therefore, coincides with their production, both with *what* they produce and with *how* they produce. Hence what individuals are depends on the material conditions of production (CW 5.31–2).

It is not consciousness that determines life, but life that determines consciousness (CW 5.37).

It is not the consciousness of men that determines their being, but, on the contrary, their social being that determines their consciousness (SW 181).

In the development of productive forces there comes a stage when productive forces and means of intercourse are brought into being which, under the existing relations, only cause mischief, and are no longer productive but destructive forces... (CW 5.52).

From forms of development of the productive forces these relations turn into their fetters. Then begins an epoch of social revolution (SW 181–2).

...the communist revolution is directed against the hitherto existing *mode* of activity, does away with *labour* [as 'a particular, exclusive sphere of activity']... The revolution is necessary, therefore, not only because the *ruling* class cannot be overthrown in any other way, but also because the class *overthrowing* it can only in a revolution succeed in ridding itself of all the muck of ages... (CW 5.47, 52–3).

With the change of the economic foundation the entire immense superstructure is more or less rapidly transformed (SW 182).

This conception of history thus relies on expounding the real process of production – starting from the material production of life itself – and comprehending the form of intercourse connected with and created by this mode of production, i.e., civil society in its various stages, as the basis of all history; describing it in its action as the state, and also explaining how all the different theoretical products and forms of consciousness, religion, philosophy, morality, etc., arise from it, and tracing the process of their formation from that basis... (CW 5.53).

In considering such transformations a distinction should always be made between the material transformation of the economic conditions of production, which can be determined with the precision of natural science, and the legal, political, religious, aesthetic or philosophic – in short, ideological forms in which men become conscious of this conflict and fight it out. Just as our opinion of an individual is not based on what he thinks of himself, so can we not judge of such a period of transformation by its own consciousness; on the contrary, this consciousness must be explained rather from the contradictions of material life, from the existing conflict between the social productive forces and the relations of production (SW 182).

Communism is not for us a *state of affairs* which is to be established, an *ideal* to which reality [will] have to adjust itself. We call communism the *real* movement which abolishes the present state of things... And if these material elements of a complete revolution are not present – namely, on the one hand the existing productive forces, on the other the formation of a revolutionary mass... then it is absolutely immaterial for practical development whether the *idea* of this revolution has been expressed a hundred times already... (CW 5.49, 54).

No social order ever perishes before all the productive forces for which there is room in it have developed; and new, higher relations of production never appear before the material conditions of their existence have matured in the womb of the old society itself. Therefore mankind always sets itself only such tasks as it can solve; since, looking at the matter more closely, it will always be found that the task itself arises only when the material conditions for its solution already exist or are at least in the process of formation (SW 182).

The first form of property is tribal property... The second form is the ancient communal and state property... The third form is feudal or estate property... The expansion of commerce and manufacture accelerated the accumulation of movable capital... created the big bourgeoisie (CW 5.32–3, 69–70).

In broad outlines Asiatic, ancient, feudal, and modern bourgeois modes of production can be designated progressive epochs in the economic formation of society (SW 182).

... connected with this [development of productive forces] a class is called forth which has to bear all the burdens of society without enjoying its advantages, which is ousted from society and forced into the sharpest contradiction to all other classes; a class which forms the majority of all members of society, and from which emanates the consciousness of the necessity of a fundamental revolution, the communist consciousness, which may, of course, arise among the other classes too through the contemplation of the situation of this class... The bourgeoisie itself develops only gradually together with its conditions, splits according to the division of labour into various sections and finally absorbs all propertied classes it finds in existence... The separate individuals form a class only insofar as they have to carry on a common battle against another class; in other respects they are on hostile terms with each other as competitors. On the other hand, the class in its turn assumes an independent existence as against the individuals,

The bourgeois relations of production are the last antagonistic form of the social process of production – antagonistic not in the sense of individual antagonism but of one arising from the social conditions of life of the individuals; at the same time the productive forces developing in the womb of bourgeois society create the material conditions for the solution of that antagonism. This social formation brings, therefore, the prehistory of human society to a close (SW 182).

so that the latter find their conditions of life predetermined, and
have their position in life and
hence their personal development assigned to them by their
class, thus becoming subsumed
under it. This is the same phenomenon as the subjection of the
separate individuals to the division of labour and can only be
removed by the abolition of private property and of labour itself
(CW 5.52, 77).

The following summary of Marx's 'outlook' from *The
German Ideology* is arguably very much plainer that the terse
phrases of the 1859 Preface, since in the earlier text mode of
production, interests, social relations, alienation, institutions
and ideology are linked together in the very questions to which
the 'guiding thread' is the answer:

How is it that personal interests always develop, against the will of
individuals, into class interests, into common interests which acquire
independent existence in relation to the individual persons, and in
their independence assume the form of *general* interests? How is it
that as such they come into contradiction with the actual individuals
and in this contradiction, by which they are defined as *general*
interests, they can be conceived by consciousness as *ideal* and even as
religious . . . interests? How is it that in this process of private interests
acquiring independent existence as class interests the personal
behaviour of the individual is bound to be objectified, estranged, and
at the same time exists as a power independent of him and without
him, created by intercourse, and is transformed into social relations,
into a series of powers which determine and subordinate the
individual . . . ? The fact [is] that within the framework of definite
modes of production, which, of course, are not dependent on the will,
alien practical forces, which are independent not only of isolated
individuals but even of all of them together, always come to stand
above people (CW 5.245).

Marx's 'guiding thread' of 1859 reproduced the premises
and social theory of *The German Ideology* without any
significant discrepancy. Marx, as he stated in his autobio-

graphical sketch, achieved 'self-clarification' in 1845, without any mention of radical departure from previous work, just as I have argued. Moreover his 'outlook' remained constant throughout his work in *Capital* and associated manuscripts.

There are, however, slight differences between the 1859 Preface and *The German Ideology* worth noting; not all the differences are really to the advantage of the later text, which suffers acutely from compression, lack of empirical illustration, proliferation of apparent synonyms and/or undefined distinctions, and the introduction of a less than successful metaphor – foundation/superstructure – which has been promoted by commentators to a position superior to the terms to which it (very roughly) refers. *The German Ideology*, as one would expect of a text left unfinished and unedited by the authors, suffers greatly from disorganised presentation and somewhat rambling generalisations, but the investigative character of the authors' work, their involvement with historical and contemporary events, their rejection of a philosophy of history and their overt political purposes are all very much clearer. The concept of class, which was merely implied in the 1859 'guiding thread' (possibly to avoid offending a censor and/or an academic audience), received much more informative treatment in *The German Ideology*, as it did in the Communist Manifesto, which is probably a good compromise between the relative advantages and disadvantages of the 1845–6 and 1859 versions of the new outlook.

Within *The German Ideology* itself the emphasis on history – a view of it, the activity of writing it – probably arose from Engels's historical work and his intention to proceed with a social history of industrial England; the attacks on idealist philosophy, historiography and politics derive very largely from Marx's determination to stamp out misleading views in Germany in order to prepare the way for his critical treatment of political economy and socialism. These are speculations, however, as with few exceptions the actual text of *The German Ideology* cannot be assigned to one writer or the other. While the manuscript is largely in Engels's hand, it is generally assumed that, at some points anyway, he acted as an amanuensis for Marx, whose handwriting was poor; Joseph Wedemeyer, a fellow communist, seems to have performed a similar function in places, though it would be rash to assign even those passages exclusively to Marx, since a process of joint composition was surely possible and indeed most likely. Whether Engels achieved the same 'self-clarification' as Marx is rather more obscure, since succeeding chapters of the present work will reveal a discrepancy between his later views and the outlook of *The German Ideology*, the 1859 Preface and Marx's work in *Capital*, despite Engels's claim that he was merely summarising this material.

The Communist Manifesto represents the most influential, readable and politically accessible of the three important joint works by Marx and Engels. It was in a sense very largely Engels's work and was almost the last one to demonstrate unambiguously his authorial virtues. While Engels had criticised Christians, conservatives, and Hegelians Old and Young, he never wrote critiques with the theoretical complexity and sophistication shown by Marx. It was rather in his empirical, economic, historical and political work of 1843–5 that he put real distance between himself and his former Young Hegelian associates. Much of the complex analysis by Marx found in the *Deutsch-Französische Jahrbücher* articles and the *Theses on Feuerbach* was not specifically reproduced in the Communist Manifesto, though there are no real discrepancies. What appears in the later text derives more from Engels's 'Outlines', *Condition of the Working Class in England*, his material on industrial development in England and Germany, and his political emphasis on class struggle as revealed in the 'Speeches in Elberfeld'. Moreover the sections on socialism can be linked to work done by Engels on Fourier, True Socialism and the *Library of the Best Foreign Socialist Writers* (in German translation) promoted by Engels to Marx, but never completed by either (CW 4.697 n. 89; 5.607 n. 144).

The level of the Communist Manifesto was very much that of the 'Speeches in Elberfeld', though the material was presented rather differently when aimed at communists rather than the middle classes. The Communist Manifesto was innocent of Marx's more abstruse analyses of idealist and realist ontology, the ultimate contradictions of the liberal state, and the peculiar nature of ideological consciousness; references to this material were brief and to the point. How different the Communist Manifesto would have been if Marx's highly theoretical elaborations – such as the examples quoted below – had intruded. While I do not mean to imply that Engels restrained Marx, who probably had no intention of writing that type of material into a popular work, it does seem that Marx was either so thoroughly adept with Engels's material that Engels himself was superfluous, or (more plausibly) that Engels and his works played a preponderant role in the making of the Communist Manifesto. This sort of discussion by Marx is notably absent from the Manifesto:

German philosophy of law and state is the only *German history* which is *al pari* with the *official* modern reality. The German nation must therefore take into account not only its present conditions but also its dream-history, and subject to criticism not only these existing conditions but at the same time their abstract continuation. Its future cannot be *limited* either to the immediate negation of its real conditions of state and law or to the immediate implementation of its ideal state and legal conditions, for it has the immediate negation of its real conditions in its ideal conditions, and it has almost *outlived* the immediate implementation of its ideal conditions in the contemplation of neighbouring nations. Hence it is with good reason that the *practical* political party in Germany demands the *negation of philosophy* (CW 3.180).

If from real apples, pears, strawberries and almonds I form the general idea '*Fruit*', if I go further and *imagine* that my abstract idea '*Fruit*', derived from real fruit, is an entity existing outside me, is indeed the *true* essence of the pear, the apple, etc., then – in the *language of speculative* philosophy – I am declaring that '*Fruit*' is the '*Substance*' of the pear, the apple, the almond, etc. . . . My finite understanding supported by my senses does of course *distinguish* an apple from a pear and a pear from an almond, but my speculative reason declares these sensuous differences inessential and irrelevant . . . Particular real fruits are no more than *semblances* whose true essence is '*the* substance' – '*Fruit*' (CW 4.57–8).

The state of affairs in Germany at the end of the last century is fully reflected in Kant's *Kritik der praktischen Vernunft* . . . Kant was satisfied with 'good will' alone, even if it remained entirely without result, and he transferred the *realisation* of this good will, the harmony between it and the needs and impulses of individuals, to *the world beyond*. Kant's good will fully corresponds to the impotence,

depression and wretchedness of the German burghers...
(CW 5.193).

Economists have a singular method of procedure. There are only two
kinds of institutions for them, artificial and natural. The institutions
of feudalism are artificial institutions, those of the bourgeoisie are
natural institutions. In this they resemble the theologians, who
likewise establish two kinds of religion. Every religion which is not
theirs is an invention of men, while their own is an emanation from
God (CW 6.174).

Marx and Engels' Euro-centric view of the 'history of all
hitherto existing society', as they presented it in the Communist
Manifesto, can be traced to Engels's 'Condition of England'
articles written (independently of Marx) in early 1844 and
published in Paris where Marx could certainly have read them
later that year. 'On the Continent too there have been poverty,
misery and social oppression... The misery and poverty of the
working class in present day England has national and even
world-historical importance.' The Reformation, Engels continued, 'brought about a major social change, the transformation of serfs into "free" workers' (CW 3.474). There are
striking parallels between Engels's 'Condition of England'
articles and the Communist Manifesto, jointly written in
1847–48:

'Condition of England' (1844)	Communist Manifesto (1847–8)
The abolition of feudal servitude has made 'cash-payment the sole relation of human beings'. Property, a natural, spiritless principle, as opposed to the human and spiritual principle, is thus enthroned, and ultimately, to complete this alienation, money – the alienated, empty abstraction of property – is made master of the world. Man has ceased to be the slave of men and has become the slave of *things*; the perversion of the human condition is complete; the	The bourgeoisie, wherever it has got the upper hand, has put an end to all feudal, patriarchal, idyllic relations. It has pitilessly torn asunder the motley feudal ties that bound man to his 'natural superiors', and has left remaining no other nexus between man and man than naked self-interest, than callous 'cash payment'. It has drowned the most heavenly ecstacies of religious fervour, of chivalrous enthusiasm, of philistine sentimentalism, in the icy water of egot-

servitude of the modern commercial world, this highly developed, total, universal venality, is more inhuman and more all-embracing than the serfdom of the feudal era; prostitution is more immoral and more bestial than the *jus primae noctis* ... all personal and national intercourse was reduced to commercial intercourse, and – which amounts to the same thing – property, things, became master of the world (CW 3.476, 485).

istical calculation. It has resolved personal worth into exchange value, and in place of the numberless indefeasible chartered freedoms, has set up that single, unconscionable freedom – Free Trade. In one word, for exploitation, veiled by religious and political illusions, it has substituted naked, shameless, direct, brutal exploitation.

The bourgeoisie has stripped of its halo every occupation hitherto honoured and looked up to with reverent awe. It has converted the physician, the lawyer, the priest, the poet, the man of science, into its paid wage-labourers (CW 6.486–7).

The sixteenth and seventeenth centuries had brought into being all the preconditions for social revolution, they had destroyed the Middle Ages, established social, political and religious Protestantism, created England's colonies, sea-power and trade, and set up alongside the aristocracy a growing and already quite powerful middle class. Social conditions gradually settled down after the disturbances of the seventeenth century and acquired a stable form which they retained until about 1780 or 1790 (CW 3.476–7).

From the serfs of the Middle Ages sprang the chartered burghers of the earliest towns. From these burgesses the first elements of the bourgeoisie were developed.

The discovery of America, the rounding of the Cape, opened up fresh ground for the rising bourgeoisie. The East-Indian and Chinese markets, the colonisation of America, trade with the colonies, the increase in the means of exchange and in commodities generally, gave to commerce, to navigation, to industry, an impulse never before known, and thereby, to the revolutionary element in the tottering feudal society, a rapid development (CW 6.485).

The consequences of an industrial impetus, once given, are

The bourgeoisie cannot exist without constantly revolutionising

endless. The progress made in one industry is communicated to all the others. The newly-created forces demand nourishment, as we have just seen; the newly-created working population brings in its wake new conditions of life and new needs. The mechanical advantages of factory production reduce the price of manufactured articles, and therefore make the necessities of life and in consequence wages in general cheaper; all other products can be sold more cheaply and thereby reach a wider market in proportion to their cheapness. Once the advantageous application of mechanical devices has been demonstrated, it is gradually imitated throughout industry; the advance in civilisation, which is the inevitable consequence of all industrial improvements, generates new needs, new industries and thus again new improvements...we shall see everywhere that the introduction of mechanical devices and of scientific principles in general has been the mainspring of progress (CW 3.482–3).

the instruments of production, and thereby the relations of production, and with them the whole relations of society. Conservation of the old modes of production in unaltered form, was, on the contrary, the first condition of existence for all earlier industrial classes. Constant revolutionising of production, uninterrupted disturbance of all social conditions, everlasting uncertainty and agitation distinguish the bourgeois epoch from all earlier ones. All fixed, fast-frozen relations, with their train of ancient and venerable prejudices and opinions, are swept away, all new-formed ones become antiquated before they can ossify. All that is solid melts into air, all that is holy is profaned, and man is at last compelled to face with sober senses, his real conditions of life, and his relations with his kind (CW 6.487).

These four industries [cotton, wool, linen, silk] which produce yarn and fabrics were thus totally revolutionised. Domestic industry was replace by collective labour in large buildings; manual labour was supplanted by steam-power and the use of machinery. With the aid of the machine a child of eight was now able to produce more than twenty

The less the skill and exertion of strength implied in manual labour, in other words, the more modern industry becomes developed, the more is the labour of men superseded by that of women. Differences of age and sex have no longer any distinctive social validity for the working class. All are instruments of labour, more or less expensive to

grown men before. Six hundred thousand factory workers, of whom half are children and more than half female, are doing the work of one hundred and fifty million people (CW 3.482).

The most immediate consequence of the creation of industry was the improvement of the means of communication. In the last century the roads in England were just as bad as elsewhere and remained so until the celebrated McAdam based road-building on scientific principles and thereby gave a new impetus to the advance of civilisation. From 1818 to 1829 new highways with a total length of 1,000 English miles were laid down in England and Wales, not counting smaller country lanes, and almost all the old roads were reconstructed according to McAdam's principles. In Scotland the public works authorities have built over 1,000 bridges since 1803. In Ireland, the wide, desolate bogs of the south, inhabited by half-wild robbers, were traversed by roads. By these means the remotest localities in the country, which had previously had no contact with the outside world, were now made accessible; in particular the Celtic-speaking areas of Wales, the Scottish Highlands and the south of Ireland were thereby compelled to make acquaintance with the outside world and accept the civilisation imposed upon them (CW 3.484).

use, according to their age and sex (CW 6.491).

The bourgeoisie, by the rapid improvement of all instruments of production, by the immensely facilitated means of communication, draws all, even the most barbarian, nations into civilisation. The cheap prices of its commodities are the heavy artillery with which it batters down all Chinese walls, with which it forces the barbarians' intensely obstinate hatred of foreigners to capitulate. It compels all nations, on pain of extinction, to adopt the bourgeois mode of production; it compels them to introduce what it calls civilisation into their midst, i.e., to become bourgeois themselves. In one word, it creates a world after its own image.

The bourgeoisie has subjected the country to the rule of the towns. It has created enormous cities, has greatly increased the urban population as compared with the rural, and has thus rescued a considerable part of the population from the idiocy of rural life. Just as it has made the country dependent on the towns, so it has made barbarian and semi-barbarian countries dependent on the civilised ones, nations of peasants on nations of bourgeois, the East on the West (CW 6.488).

The nature and origin of the bourgeoisie, its effect on preceding social relations, its role in mechanising production and altering working conditions, and finally the imperial character of capitalist production are all features of the Communist Manifesto mirroring Engels's early articles. In Marx's early works these developments were not treated in the detailed yet sweeping way characteristic of Engels; conversely, the early Marx on alienation and emancipation was visible by implication (not through explicit use of text) in the Manifesto as published.

Further passages in the Communist Manifesto can be traced to Engels's 'Outlines of a Critique of Political Economy' (on free competition), his *Condition of the Working Class in England* (on the family), and the 'Speeches in Elberfeld' (on the abolition of private property). Engels had made these topics his own in a way that Marx had not. Parallels between the Communist Manifesto and the jointly written *German Ideology* could be established with little difficulty, since the historical development of bourgeois from feudal society was extensively treated in the earlier text, but then that topic, as I have already suggested, was not one of Marx's real preoccupations but was rather Engels's project at the time, in so far as he had one. Marx's focus was on establishing the reality of class struggle, what in general terms underlay it, and how capitalism generated a particularly virulent form of social oppression.

The Communist Manifesto leads the reader straight into the class struggle. This was characteristic of Engels's revolutionary political perspective, which dates back to his predictions in late 1842 of 'inevitable' revolution in England mentioned in the articles he wrote on his early visit there, some two years before his association with Marx began (CW 2.374). The genre of the Manifesto and its agitational character were much closer to Engels's work than to Marx's more theoretically specialised and therefore more limited efforts, in terms of potential political effect. The Manifesto developed from Engels's attempts to draft a programme to which communists could *adhere*; most of Marx's energies went into minatory effusions on what views everyone should *avoid*.

While in Brussels, Marx and Engels organised a 'correspondence committee' to put French, English and German

Socialists (particularly émigrés) in touch as 'a step which the social movement should take in its *literary* expression in order to free itself of its *national* limitations' (SC 28). The remnants of the League of the Just, now in London, once more approached Marx to offer him membership; Marx and Engels joined in early 1847, in expectation of a congress which was duly held in London in June that year (McLellan (1973), 171–2). Engels attended and prepared for the newly renamed Communist League a 'Draft of a Communist Confession of Faith' for circulation; a second draft, 'Principles of Communism', was written in October for consideration at the second congress in November/December, which apparently authorised Marx and Engels to produce a final version. They worked together in December 1847, and Marx finished the manuscript at the end of January 1848 for publication in London (in German) the following month. However, Engels wrote to Marx that he was unhappy about the catechistic form he had adopted, because 'more or less history must be narrated'; hence it should be entitled 'Communist *Manifesto*' (MEW 27.107).

Marx's final version, in overall structure and content, was a rewritten version of Engels's draft, somewhat edited down (as in Engels's lengthy views on communist society), rearranged and occasionally expanded. It included more discussion of trades unions, the downs as well as ups of class struggle ('the workers are victorious, but only for a time'), and new passages on the relationship between communists and proletarians (CW 6.493). Marx seems to have shifted the focus from England to Germany in a way that suggested a more sophisticated grasp of the interaction between industrial and political forces than Engels possessed or at least had committed to paper. Engels wrote that revolution would 'develop more quickly or more slowly according to whether the country has a more developed industry'; revolution 'will therefore be slowest and most difficult to carry out in Germany, quickest and easiest in England' (CW 6.352). The final version suggested that Germany 'is on the eve of a bourgeois revolution that is bound to be carried out under more advanced conditions, . . . and with a much more developed proletariat, than that of England was in the seventeenth, and of France in the eighteenth century'

(CW 6.519). Engels linked industrial development and revolution in a more straightforward way than Marx, but this hardly makes his view 'determinist', as some commentators have claimed. Marx may of course have been appeasing Germans in the League (which was principally German, anyway), who might have felt consigned to a revolutionary backwater by Engels's Anglo-centric view. In what sense the German proletariat was more developed was not specified by Marx, but he was presumably referring to a revolutionary consciousness purged of the religious, utopian and parliamentary illusions characteristic of the English and French workers' movements. That sort of conclusion would follow from Marx's dedication to such a theoretical project, even if the empirical evidence for such development were not forthcoming. Engels's brief comments on rival 'so-called socialists' were greatly expanded by Marx in the section 'Socialist and Communist Literature'; on that sort of critique he was indubitably in the lead.

Engels later said that the Communist Manifesto was essentially Marx's work, a statement made in a short biography of Marx published in 1869 just after the publication of volume one of *Capital* when Marx needed publicity (MEW 16.363). The Manifesto itself had long been out of print in Germany, and was presumably not the sort of item to which Engels would have clung to bolster his own reputation, which at this period was not at all an issue. In the sense that Marx was responsible for the narrative flow of the Manifesto in its final version, the work was essentially his. But in so far as the historical development of capitalism, its contemporary functioning in England, and a crucial political emphasis on the class struggle were concerned, Engels's work was highly relevant to Marx's composition. The 'Principles of Communism' by Engels confirms this analysis, as it is obviously a rough draft of the Manifesto as we know it. An extended comparison of the two texts reveals that the major points of the Communist Manifesto were drafted in Engels's 'Principles' and that Marx's effort on the text was essentially, though rather heavily, editorial:

'Principles of Communism'

Communist Manifesto

Depending on the different stages of the development of society, the working classes . . . stood in different relations to the possessing and ruling classes. In ancient times the working people were the *slaves* of their owners . . . In the Middle Ages they were the *serfs* of the landowning nobility, just as they still are in Hungary, Poland, and Russia. In the Middle Ages and up to the industrial revolution there were in the towns also journeymen . . . (CW 6.343).

In the earlier epochs of history, we find almost everywhere a complicated arrangement of society into various orders, a manifold gradation of social rank. In ancient Rome we have patricians, knights, plebeians, slaves; in the Middle Ages, feudal lords, vassals, guild-masters, journeymen, apprentices, serfs; in almost all of these classes again, subordinate gradations (CW 6.482–5).

Owing to the continual cheapening of the price of industrial products as a result of machine labour, the old system of manufacture or industry founded upon manual labour was completely destroyed in all countries of the world. All semi-barbarian countries, which until now had been more or less outside historical development and whose industry had until now been based on manufacture, were thus forcibly torn out of their isolation . . . Thus countries that for thousands of years had made no progress, for example India, were revolutionised through and through, and even China is now marching towards a revolution. It has reached the point that a new machine invented today in England, throws millions of workers in China out of work within a year. Large-

The feudal system of industry, under which industrial production was monopolised by closed guilds, now no longer sufficed for the growing wants of the new markets. The manufacturing system took its place. The guild-masters were pushed on one side by the manufacturing middle class; division of labour between the different corporate guilds vanished in the face of division of labour in each single workshop.

Meantime the markets kept ever growing, the demand ever rising. Even manufacture no longer sufficed. Thereupon, steam and machinery revolutionised industrial production . . . Modern industry has established the world market, for which the discovery of America paved the way. This market has given an immense development to com-

scale industry has thus brought all the peoples of the earth into relationship with one another, thrown all the small local markets into the world market, prepared the way everywhere for civilisation and progress, and brought it about that everything that happens in the civilised countries must have its repercussions on all other countries (CW 6.345).

The bourgeoisie having thus annihilated the social power of the nobility and the guild-burghers, annihilated their political power as well. Having become the first class in society, the bourgeoisie proclaimed itself also the first class in the political sphere. It did this by establishing the representative system, which rests upon bourgeois equality before the law and the legal recognition of free competition, and which in European countries was introduced in the form of constitutional monarchy. Under these constitutional monarchies those only are electors who possess a certain amount of capital, that is to say, the bourgeois; these bourgeois electors elect the deputies, and these bourgeois deputies, by means of the right to refuse taxes, elect a bourgeois government (CW 6.346).

With this facility of production

merce, to navigation, to communication by land. This development has, in its turn, reacted on the extension of industry; and in proportion as industry, commerce, navigation, railways extended, in the same proportion the bourgeoisie developed, increased its capital, and pushed into the background every class handed down from the Middle Ages (CW 6.485–6).

Each step in the development of the bourgeoisie was accompanied by a corresponding political advance of that class. An oppressed class under the sway of the feudal nobility, an armed and self-governing association in the medieval commune; here independent urban republic (as in Italy and Germany), there taxable 'third estate' of the monarchy (as in France), afterwards, in the period of manufacture proper, serving either the semi-feudal or the absolute monarchy as a counterpoise against the nobility, and, in fact, cornerstone of the great monarchies in general, the bourgeoisie has at last, since the establishment of Modern Industry and of the world market, conquered for itself, in the modern representative State, exclusive political sway. The executive of the modern State is but a committee for managing the common affairs of the whole bourgeoisie (CW 6.486).

It is enough to mention the

the free competition necessarily resulting from large-scale industry very soon assumed an extremely intense character; numbers of capitalists launched into industry, and very soon more was being produced than could be used. The result was that the goods manufactured could not be sold, and a so-called trade crisis ensued. Factories had to stand idle, factory owners went bankrupt, and the workers lost their bread. Everywhere there was the greatest misery. After a while the surplus products were sold, the factories started working again, wages went up, and gradually business was more brisk than ever. But before long too many commodities were again produced, another crisis ensued, and ran the same course as the previous one. Thus since the beginning of this century the state of industry has continually fluctuated between periods of prosperity and periods of crisis, and almost regularly every five to seven years a similar crisis has occurred, and every time it has entailed the greatest misery for the workers, general revolutionary ferment, and the greatest danger to the entire existing system... Although in the initial stages of its development large-scale industry itself created free competition, it has now nevertheless outgrown free competition; that competition and in general the carrying on of industrial production by indi-

commercial crisis that by their periodical return put on its trial, each time more threateningly, the existence of the entire bourgeois society. In these crises a great part not only of the existing products, but also of the previously created productive forces, are periodically destroyed. In these crises there breaks out an epidemic that, in all earlier epochs, would have seemed an absurdity – the epidemic of overproduction. Society suddenly finds itself put back into a state of momentary barbarism; it appears as if a famine, a universal war of devastation had cut off the supply of every means of subsistence; industry and commerce seem to be destroyed; and why? Because there is too much civilisation, too much means of subsistence, too much industry, too much commerce. The productive forces at the disposal of society no longer tend to further the development of the conditions of bourgeois property; on the contrary, they have become too powerful for these conditions, by which they are fettered, and so soon as they overcome these fetters, they bring disorder into the whole of bourgeois society, endanger the existence of bourgeois property. The conditions of bourgeois society are too narrow to comprise the wealth created by them. And how does the bourgeoisie get over these crisis? On the one hand by enforced destruction of a mass of productive forces; on the other,

viduals have become a fetter upon large-scale industry which it must and will break; that large-scale industry, so long as it is conducted on its present basis, can only survive through a general confusion repeating itself every seven years which each time threatens all civilisation, not merely plunging the proletarians into misery but also ruining a great number of bourgeois... (CW 6.347).

by the conquest of new markets, and by the more thorough exploitation of the old ones. That is to say, by paving the way for more extensive and more destructive crises, and by diminishing the means whereby crises are prevented... But not only has the bourgeoisie forged the weapons that bring death to itself; it has also called into existence the men who are to wield those weapons – the modern working class – the proletarians (CW 6.489–90).

The price of labour is, therefore, likewise equal to the cost of production of labour. The cost of production of labour consists precisely of the amount of the means of subsistence required for the worker to maintain himself in a condition in which he is capable of working and to prevent the working class from dying out (CW 6.343).

The average price of wage-labour is the minimum wage, *i.e.*, that quantum of the means of subsistence, which is absolutely requisite to keep the labourer in bare existence as a labourer. What, therefore, the wage-labourer appropriates by means of his labour, merely suffices to prolong and reproduce a bare existence (CW 6.499).

What influence will the communist order of society have upon the family?

It will make the relation between the sexes a purely private relation which concerns only the persons involved, and in which society has no call to interfere. It is able to do this because it abolishes private property and educates children communally, thus destroying the twin foundation of hitherto existing marriage – the dependence through private property of the

The bourgeois clap-trap about the family and education, about the hallowed co-relation of parent and child, becomes all the more disgusting, the more, by the action of Modern Industry, all family ties among the proletarians are torn asunder, and their children transformed into simple articles of commerce and instruments of labour.

But you Communists would introduce community of women, screams the whole bourgeoisie in chorus... Bourgeois marriage is

wife upon the husband and of the children upon the parents. Here also is the answer to the outcry of moralising philistines against the communist community of women. Community of women is a relationship that belongs altogether to bourgeois society and is completely realised today in prostitution. But prostitution is rooted in private property and falls with it. Thus instead of introducing the community of women, communist organisation puts an end to it (CW 6.354).

in reality a system of wives in common and thus, at the most, what the Communists might possibly be reproached with, is that they desire to introduce, in substitution for a hypocritically concealed, an openly legalised community of women. For the rest, it is self-evident that the abolition of the present system of production must bring with it the abolition of the community of women springing from that system, *i.e.*, of prostitution both public and private (CW 6.502).

Education will enable young people quickly to go through the whole system of production, it will enable them to pass from one branch of industry to another according to the needs of society or their own inclinations. It will therefore free them from that one-sidedness which the present division of labour stamps on each one of them. Thus the communist organisation of society will give its members the chance of an all-round exercise of abilities that have received all-round development (CW 6.353).

And your education! Is not that also social, and determined by the social conditions under which you educate, by the intervention, direct or indirect of society, by means of schools, etc.? The Communists have not invented the intervention of society in education; they do but seek to alter the character of that intervention, and to rescue education from the influence of the ruling class (CW 6.502).

Democracy would be quite useless to the proletariat if it were not immediately used as a means of carrying through further measures directly attacking private ownership and securing the means of subsistence of the proletariat. Chief among these measures, already made necessary by the existing conditions, are the following:

We have seen above, that the first step in the revolution by the working class is to raise the proletariat to the position of ruling class, to win the battle of democracy... In the beginning, this cannot be effected except by means of despotic inroads on the rights of property... In the most advanced countries, the following will be pretty generally ap-

1. Limitation of private ownership by means of progressive taxation, high inheritance taxes....
2. Gradual expropriation of landed proprietors, factory owners, railway and shipping magnates....
3. Confiscation of the property of all emigrants and rebels....
4. Organisation of the labour or employment of the proletarians on national estates, in national factories and workshops....
5. Equal liability to work for all members of society until complete abolition of private ownership. Formation of industrial armies, especially for agriculture.
6. Centralisation of the credit and banking system in the hands of the State by means of a national bank with state capital....
7. Increase of national factories, workshops, railways, and ships, cultivation of all uncultivated land and improvement of land already cultivated....
8. Education of all children... combined with production.
9. The erection of large palaces on national estates as common dwellings for communities of citizens engaged in industry as well as agriculture, and combining the advantages of both urban and rural life without the one-sidedness and disadvantages of either.
10. The demolition of all insanitary and badly built dwellings and town districts.
11. Equal right of inheritance to

plicable:
1. Abolition of property in land and application of all rents of land to public purposes.
2. A heavy progressive or graduated income tax.
3. Abolition of all right of inheritance.
4. Confiscation of the property of all emigrants and rebels.
5. Centralisation of credit in the hands of the State, by means of a national bank with State capital and an exclusive monopoly.
6. Centralisation of the means of communication and transport in the hands of the State.
7. Extension of factories and instruments of production owned by the State; the bringing into cultivation of waste-lands, and the improvement of the soil generally in accordance with a common plan.
8. Equal liability of all to labour. Establishment of industrial armies, especially for agriculture.
9. Combination of agriculture with manufacturing industries; gradual abolition of the distinction between town and country, by a more equable distribution of the population over the country.
10. Free education for all children in public schools. Abolition of children's factory labour in its present form. Combination of education with industrial production, etc., etc. (CW 6.504–5).

be enjoyed by illegitimate and legitimate children.
12. Concentration of all means of transport in the hands of the nation (CW 6.350–1).

In what way do Communists differ from socialists?
The so-called socialists fall into three groups... *reactionary* socialists... *bourgeois socialists* ... *democratic socialists* (CW 6.355).

Socialist and Communist Literature
1. Reactionary Socialism
   a. *Feudal Socialism*
   b. *Petty-Bourgeois Socialism*
   c. *German, or 'True',* *Socialism*
2. Conservative, or Bourgeois, Socialism
3. Critical-Utopian Socialism and Communism (CW 6.507–17).

In England, France, and Belgium, where the bourgeoisie rules, the Communists still have for the time being a common interest with the various democratic parties... for instance, the Chartists... In *America*... the Communists must make common cause with the party that will turn this constitution against the bourgeoisie and use it in the interests of the proletariat, that is, with the national agrarian reformers.

In *Switzerland* the radicals, although still a very mixed party, are yet the only people with whom the Communists can have anything to do... Finally, in *Germany* the decisive struggle between the bourgeoisie and the absolute monarchy is still to come... The Communists must therefore always take the side of

Section II has made clear the relations of the Communists to the existing working-class parties, such as the Chartists in England and the Agrarian Reformers in America... In France the Communists ally themselves with the Social-Democrats, against the conservative and radical bourgeoisie, reserving, however, the right to take up a critical position... In Switzerland they support the Radicals... In Poland they support the party that insists on an agrarian revolution... In Germany they fight with the bourgeoisie whenever it acts in a revolutionary way, against the absolute monarchy, the feudal squirearchy, and the petty bourgeoisie... The Communists turn their attention chiefly to Germany... because the bour-

the liberal bourgeois against the governments but they must ever be on their guard against sharing the self-deceptions of the bourgeois or believing their false assurances about the benefits which the victory of the bourgeoisie will bring to the proletariat (CW 6.356).

geois revolution in Germany will be but the prelude to an immediately following proletarian revolution (CW 6.518–19).

This comparison illustrates the overwhelming coincidence of topics between Engels's 'Principles of Communism' and the Communist Manifesto as Marx left it, as well as a general similarity in the views expressed in the two texts. The many minor differences of emphasis and detail within these broadly parallel passages ought not necessarily to be ascribed to a difference in opinion between Marx and Engels on any given point. The Communist Manifesto was written (rather hastily, as we can deduce from the way Marx was prodded to meet a deadline) to satisfy a committee whose individual and collective predilections may have been known to Marx but are not precisely available to us. Moreover Marx and Engels were apart during the final drafting, so they then had no opportunity to reconcile any differences between themselves as they might have done had they been together. In addition the text was unsigned, so it might have contained material with which the authors would not have wished personally to identify themselves without qualification, whereas adherence to a manifesto is usually compatible with individual reservations on particular points.

By the time the Marx–Engels collaboration began in November 1844 there was already a considerable degree of overlap between their two intellects in terms of interests, projects, politics and methods. Even if there were no genuine grey areas with respect to who wrote what in particular works (e.g. *The German Ideology*), it would still be difficult to assign any given idea to one or the other as if the opposite partner had never heard of it or of anything like it. What can be said is that Marx was the more penetrating theoretician, in the sense of clarifying premises held in common and distinguishing the philosophical errors of rival writers. Engels was the more impressive historian and politician. His gifts for economic analysis were superseded by Marx's overwhelming sense of vocation in pursuing a critique of political economy; and his achievements in social research were taken over, literally incorporated and gratefully acknowledged by Marx. In that way, the path Marx took on his lifework was considerably smoothed and shortened. From about 1846 Engels (sadly) did little further work in economic analysis and empirical social research, but he continued his political and historical work in the form of correspondence, journalism and meetings as well as in the various versions of the Manifesto discussed above; in the 1850s he also undertook a study of the peasant war in Germany and wrote articles for Marx about the revolutionary events of 1848–49.

In later years Engels had occasion to return in print to Marx's theoretical distinctions and self-clarifications of the highly-charged 1840s. In doing so he invented 'dialectics', the direct ancestor of Marxism, and in that way he found the vocational focus missing in his earlier career.

4 The Invention of Dialectics

The revolutionary events of 1848–49 altered the lives and circumstances of Marx and Engels, but changed their work surprisingly little. Once the hectic months of journalism were over, and the two had made their separate ways to England and exile, Marx continued his critique of political economy, tormented by poverty and the need to take paid work in journalism. His own autobiography treats 1848–49 almost as an interruption to his studies. Engels wrote *The Peasant War in Germany* during 1850 for Marx's new journal, which was short-lived as usual, and then went to work for the family firm in Manchester. He supported the Marx ménage and wrote little but occasional journalism (some of it – *Revolution and Counter-Revolution in Germany* – published under Marx's name) during the 1850s and 1860s.

One short text from this period that has received little attention is Engels's anonymous review of Marx's *A Contribution to the Critique of Political Economy* of 1859, the first instalment of the long-promised critical work. This lack of attention is unfortunate, because Engels's brief notice represents a turning point in his thought, his career and in the Marx–Engels intellectual relationship as we see it. Though its direct influence has been limited and its effect on the contemporary Marx–Engels relationship very slight (so far as we know), the text is our first actual record of an important development in Engels's ideas that presaged the most influential works of the Marxist tradition – *Anti-Dühring*, *Socialism, Utopian and Scientific*, *Ludwig Feuerbach and the End of Classical German Philosophy* – all by Engels. While socialists, communists and even self-confessed Marxists paid lip-service to the power of *Capital*, Marx's *magnum opus*, it was these works that were most widely read and whose tenets were passed on in lectures, primers and handbooks, down to official Soviet dialectics. Even more importantly, in his short review Engels initiated the Marxist philosophical tradition itself, *and* what has become the standard mould for interpreting Marx's life and thought, used by pro- and anti-Marxists and by academic commentators alike. All these developments, of incomparable significance for our social and political life today, can be traced to Engels's review of August 1859.

Marx wanted publicity for his *A Contribution to the Critique of Political Economy*, and he wrote to Engels on 19 July 1859 saying that *Das Volk* would do a review but that he did not trust the editor Eduard Biskamp, who 'knows nothing about the subject'. Marx asked if Engels could write this review, and inquired again on 22 July: 'You have forgotten to write to me whether you would do the review of my book . . . In case you do write something, don't forget 1) that Proudhonism is nipped in the bud, 2) that the character of bourgeois production, which is *specifically* social and by no means *absolute*, is analysed in its simplest form, that of the commodity'. Marx explained that 'Herr [Wilhelm] Liebknecht [fellow communist and participant in the 1848–49 events] has told Biskamp that "never has a book so *frustrated* him"', and Biskamp himself has said to me that he does not see "the good of it"'. Engels promised to do the article 'next week', because it would be 'a *job*' requiring notice – he had also seen the 'completely mangled advertisements' for the book in two newspapers, so evidently he took Marx's point with some enthusiasm (MEW 29.460, 463, 464).

Engels sent the beginning of his article to Marx on 3 August and reported on a delay on the 10th. No substantive comment (other than a plea for speed) survives in Marx's letters for the month. Engels's review appeared in two parts – a promised third section dealing with Marx's achievements in economic theory in detail never emerged.

Using the outlook of *The German Ideology*, the Communist Manifesto, and his own historical work in *The Peasant War in Germany* and *Revolution and Counter-Revolution in Germany*, Engels approached Marx's critique of political economy

through German economic history from the seventeenth
century, because 'political economy is the theoretical analysis
of modern bourgeois society and therefore presupposes
developed bourgeois conditions'. These were slow in taking
shape in Germany because of the separation of Holland and
the devastation of the civil wars. England, France and Holland
forged ahead in trade, colonisation and manufacturing, until
England alone attained the foremost position, 'owing to steam
power which only then began to impart value to its coal and
iron deposits'. No German political economy was possible,
concluded Engels, while Germans were still struggling against
'ludicrously antiquated relics of the Middle Ages' such as
customs barriers and idiotic trade regulations. Up to 1830
these circumstances 'laid fetters on the material bourgeois
development of Germany' (SW 1.366). In his Preface to the
work under review, Marx had commented on 'relations of
production' that turn from 'forms of development of productive forces . . . into their fetters' (SW 1.363). Engels was thus
preparing his readers for Marx's 'guiding thread', which he
quoted explicitly, and for Marx's critique, which he identified
as the 'scientific, independent *German economics*' dating
precisely, so Engels said, from the (unspecified) moment when
'the German proletarian party appeared on the scene'
(SW 1.368).

In the 1859 review Engels described Marx's economics as
new because it 'is grounded essentially upon the *materialist
conception of history*', the first usage of this phrase. Marx had
made a revolutionising discovery which Engels quoted from
the Preface: '"the mode of production of material life conditions the social, political and intellectual life process in
general"'. This was applicable, according to Engels, not merely
to economics but to 'all historical sciences', by which he
presumably meant social sciences, since he claimed, somewhat
mysteriously, that 'all sciences which are not natural sciences
are historical' (SW 1.368). (Physics and chemistry might count
as non-historical natural sciences, unlike geology and natural
history – which are historical, though not about society.)

Even more curiously Engels wrote that the basic proposition
of this 'materialist conception of history' is 'so simple that it
must be self-evident': this proposition was Marx's very general

summary that '"it is not the consciousness of men that determines their being, but their social being that determines their
consciousness"'. For Engels the value of this discovery lay in
comprehending and *deriving* truths about any society in history.
In his view, Marx's proposition meant 'that all the social and
political relations, all religious and legal systems, all the
theoretical outlooks which emerge in history, are to be
comprehended only when the material conditions of life of the
respectively corresponding epochs are understood and the
former are derived from these material conditions'. Moreover
his notion of what to do with Marx's insight was at an
obviously academic remove from the actual politics of their
party, though he claimed somewhat vaguely that 'the basic
outlook runs like a red thread' through all its 'literary
productions'. Engels suggested that the real scientific work to
be done (which demanded 'years of tranquil study') was the
development of the materialist conception with respect to
historical examples. He dealt with the *practical* consequences of
the materialist conception of history in a summary manner,
merely quoting the passage from Marx's 'guiding thread' on
social revolution. Yet even that was presented by Engels as a
'perspective' that 'unfolds itself before us' (SW 1.368–9).

The intention of Engels's remark that the materialist conception of history is 'self-evident' was to ridicule those
'bemused by idealist delusions'. Idealism was then his chosen
target, though he did not explain precisely why he was
attacking a philosophical doctrine as such. What he did claim is
that the new outlook 'runs directly counter to all idealism, even
the most concealed'. Evidently the 'whole traditional mode of
political reasoning', the 'representatives of the bourgeoisie',
the 'French Socialists' and the 'German vulgar-democratic
vociferators', so Engels claimed, participated in idealist delusions and had, at the same time 'attempted to exploit
[Marx's] new ideas in plagiaristic fashion'. Philosophical
idealists, it seems, had some of the same characteristics for
Engels as 'our party': both made their marks, depending on
circumstances, in the study and on the political stage
(SW 1.368–9). Moreover the new treatment of economics bore
another important similarity to the great works of idealist
philosophers. To develop that point Engels appealed explicitly

to Hegel. This tradition – that one approaches Marx's work through a study of Hegel – was first established in Engels's review.

Engels took Marx's mature critique of political economy (the first published portion of which was the 1859 *Contribution to the Critique of Political Economy* under review) to be 'a systematic integration of the whole complex of economic science [and]... at the same time a criticism of the whole of economic literature'. Then Engels implied that Hegel's work (without specifying any particular books at this stage) was the model for this kind of enterprise – the development of 'a science in its own inner interconnection' (SW 1.370). Hegel's own approach to philosophy and logic might have served Engels in developing this alleged analogy with Marx, since Hegel's *Science of Logic*, for example, presents a systematic account of logic as a whole, with Hegel's own critical improvements and philosophical gloss on the works of other authorities.

Instead of establishing his case with respect to Hegel and Marx, Engels rushed to ridicule the 'official Hegelian school' which 'had appropriated from the dialectic of the master only the manipulation of the simplest of all tricks'. In Engels's view the achievements of Hegel were eclipsed by the 'ludicrous clumsiness' of his followers, by the transformative criticism of Feuerbach (who 'declared speculative conceptions untenable'), and by 'the powerful bourgeois development after 1848', not least in industry and science. Engels took the approach of natural scientists to be gratifyingly non-idealist but disappointingly un-Hegelian. Their 'natural-scientific materialism' ('almost indistinguishable theoretically from that of the eighteenth century') unfortunately presupposed 'fixed categories rather than a 'speculative tendency'. A 'speculative tendency' as happily developed in idealist philosophy, was able to leap 'the ditch which separates essence from appearance, cause from effect'.

Rather eccentrically Engels referred to the un-Hegelian belief in fixed categories (a view that concepts have determinate, unvarying referents) as 'the old metaphysics'. This 'metaphysics', according to Engels, was reflected in certain philosophical works of the last century or so, notably those by

Christian Wolff (1679–1754), Ludwig Büchner (1824–99) and Jakob Moleschott (1822–93). It was also reflected in the works of 'the bourgeois economists' (including, presumably, the English and French authorities who wrote long before 1848) as well as in contemporary works by Engels's fellow-countrymen. For contemporary German attempts to contribute to economic science, which dated from the establishment of the Customs Union in 1834, Engels had nothing but the scorn he had formerly poured on German literary efforts:

Presently the learned fraternity and the bureaucracy seized hold of the imported material and worked it up in a fashion not very creditable to the 'German spirit'. From the medley of high-class swindlers, merchants, schoolmasters and bureaucrats dabbling in authorship there arose thereupon a German economic literature which in its insipidity, shallowness, lack of thought, verbosity and plagiarism was paralleled only by the German novel (SW 1.367, 370–1).

Engels dismissed the 'metaphysics' of fixed categories as 'annihilated theoretically by Kant and particularly by Hegel'. Natural scientists, philosophers and bourgeois economists had simply failed to grasp the philosophical (albeit idealist) critique of the 'wolffian-metaphysical method'. In fact, idealism fell right out of fashion, according to Engels, when 'Germany plunged into the natural sciences with quite extraordinary energy' after 1848 (SW 1.371–2). The strict correlations between economic innovation, on the one hand, and theoretical and political developments on the other, recalls the treatment of revolutionary prospects in Europe in Engels's 'Principles of Communism' (which seems to have been revised by Marx into the more subtle analysis of the Communist Manifesto).

Unsurprisingly Engels's alternative to this alleged metaphysics of fixed categories was not Hegelianism itself, because it 'was essentially idealistic', took 'pure thinking as its start', and '"came from nothing through nothing to nothing"' on its own admission (no reference was provided here by Engels). Yet logically Hegelianism was far superior to its rival, Engels argued, though 'absolutely unusable in its *available* form'. An appropriate use for the logical content of Hegelianism was in

solving this problem. 'How was science to be treated?'
(SW 1.371–2). Not, it should be noted, how was science to be
done?

What Engels had in mind was the development of 'a science
in its own inner interconnection' on the model of Hegel's
encyclopedic treatment of all the sciences of his time – philosophical, historical and natural – for which he used his
'Hegelian method' (SW 1.370, 372). Political economy was
merely one of those sciences and it had, indeed, been treated
by Hegel himself in his *Philosophy of Right*. Thus Engels's
notion of the project, for which a revised Hegelianism was
the appropriate method, was an interpretative, recapitulatory,
critical, systematic treatment of all knowledge (since, in his
view and Hegel's, knowledge of any importance coincided with
science broadly conceived, in the German manner, as
Wissenschaft). Quite what the *point* of such an encyclopedic
system would be was never demonstrated by Engels. He merely
took it that this kind of exercise would in itself contribute to
knowledge through its substantive interconnections between
laws already established, and through its formulation of the
principles that underlay the interconnections in the work itself.
Engels's view of the Marxian project was thus academic,
philosophical, even quasi-Hegelian.

The required revision of Hegelianism comprised, according
to Engels, the development of 'a world outlook more materialistic than *any* previous one [my italics]', including, presumably,
previous materialisms. Quite how this was possible was not
explained. Because of his concept of Marx's ultimate project
(or at least the project allegedly implied by Marx's critical work
on political economy), Engels assigned to Marx *a method* that
was said to be of 'hardly less importance' than his 'basic,
materialist outlook itself' (SW 1.372, 373). Method emerged
as Engels's chief concern in putting Marx's work across to
an educated public.

Once Engels had left aside (temporarily) the nature of
Marx's materialistic revision of Hegel's premises, he faced the
daunting task of showing how Marx had extracted his new
method from Hegelian logic. The 'kernel' of that dialectical
logic, according to Engels, comprises 'Hegel's real discoveries
in this sphere', and Marx aimed to 'reconstruct the dialectical

method'. Once Marx had (in an as yet unspecified way) 'divested' Hegel's method 'of its idealistic trappings', he had not merely produced, so Engels claimed, the method most suitable for developing a 'science in its own inner interconnection', but had revealed 'the simple shape in which it [the dialectical method] becomes the only true form of development of thought' (SW 1.370, 373). What this grand claim amounts to was not really specified, but it was presumably the way in which all 'science' was 'to be treated'.

However far Engels intended to push his claims concerning this revision of Hegelian method, it is clear that methodology for him was a substantial part of Marx's legacy, indeed the most substantial part, since its applicability was allegedly very wide, or possibly even universal (in some obscure sense). The 'basic materialist outlook itself' would hardly amount to much, on this view, were there no method that presupposed this ('revolutionising discovery' and actually led to results (SW 1.368, 373).

Curiously Engels fastened on the historical character of Hegel's thought as the methodological feature that distinguishes it 'from that of all other philosophers', rather than Hegel's more obviously innovative method of developing a succession of concepts, as in the *Phenomenology of Mind* (Sense-Certainty to Absolute Knowledge) and the *Science of Logic* (Being to Absolute Idea). Those two Hegelian works were the ones used by Marx in his own methodological inquiries in the *Economic and Philosophical Manuscripts* of 1844 and the *Grundrisse* notebooks of 1857–58. Nonetheless Engels was right in suggesting that Hegel's philosophy has a historical character in scope and method that set him apart from other philosophers:

... Hegel – in contrast to his disciples – did not parade ignorance, but was one of the finest intellects of all time. He was the first who attempted to show a development, an inner coherence, in history; and while today much in his philosophy of history may seem peculiar to us, yet the grandeur of his fundamental outlook is admirable even today, whether one makes comparison with his predecessors or, to be sure, with anyone who, since his time, has indulged in general reflections concerning history. Everywhere, in his *Phenomenology, Esthetics, History of Philosophy*, this magnificent conception of history prevails, and everywhere the material is treated historically, in a definite, even if abstractly distorted, interconnection with history (SW 1.372).

Engels commented further that for Hegel world history was the 'test' of his philosophical conception. Test, however, implies a criterion by which a theory should be adjusted, and this was not Hegel's view. But Engels observed with some justification that the 'real content of historical events entered everywhere into the philosophy', though he added that 'the real relation was inverted and stood on its head'. This was probably a mystifying reference by Engels to Hegel's idealism, rather than to Hegel's alleged use of history as a test (SW 1.372).

Actually Hegel argued that his account of history relied on a purely philosophical proof which was *confirmed* by all actual events – just the reverse of what Engels claimed. Hegel wrote in the *Philosophy of History* that 'the only Thought which Philosophy brings with it to the contemplation of History, is the simple conception of *Reason*'. Reason is thus 'the sovereign of the World'; and the history of the world is a 'rational process'. According to Hegel, this is a 'hypothesis in the domain of history as such', but in that of Philosophy, 'it is no hypothesis'. In Philosophy it is proved by 'speculative cognition' that Reason underlies 'all the natural and spiritual life which it originates'. This is the thesis, Hegel concluded, that 'has been proved in Philosophy', and is here in the *Philosophy of History* 'regarded as demonstrated' (Hegel (1837/1956), 9–10).

At the same time Hegel recognised the possible charge that he was merely applying *a priori* conceptions to history and thus forcing historical facts into a preconceived mould, but in his defence he appealed to natural science:

The investigator must be familiar *a priori* (if we like to call it so), with the whole circle of conceptions to which the principles in question belong – just as Kepler (to name the most illustrious example in this mode of philosophising) must have been familiar *a priori* with ellipses, with cubes and squares, and with ideas of their relations, before he could discover, from the empirical data, those immortal 'Laws' of his.

'In this very process of scientific *Understanding*', Hegel concluded, the essential must be distinguished from the 'so-called non-essential'. But in the history of the world it is the 'Consciousness of Freedom, and the phases which this consciousness assumes in developing itself', that is essential; this distinction enables the Hegelian philosopher to make a 'scientific' discrimination (Hegel (1837/1956), 63–5). Thus the history presented by Hegel was tested by philosophy, not the philosophy by history.

Engels misinterpreted Hegel's use of history in relation to his philosophical conception. The philosophical conception was, in Hegel's eyes, proved already, and historical events merely confirmed this. But having introduced Hegel's conception of the relation between philosophy and history (albeit erroneously), Engels created two problems for himself: the substitution for Hegel's premised idealism of a 'world outlook' that was 'more materialistic'; and the delineation of the correct relationship between historical events and their 'reflection' in 'abstract and theoretically consistent form' (as allegedly found in Marx's work) (SW 1.372–3). Once those problems were solved to his satisfaction, Engels could then progress in his 1859 review to the method used by Marx. This was the method, so Engels claimed, for presenting scientifically, that is materialistically, logically and dialectically, a given social relation in its historical context.

By remarking that in Hegel's idealist philosophy 'the real relation was inverted and stood on its head', Engels the materialist made himself less than clear, since he failed to specify the terms of the relation and the way that they were related so that we could know what was inverted and what was stood on its head. The inversion metaphor derives from Feuerbachian criticism of Hegel and was employed by Engels in his 'Outlines of a Critique of Political Economy' written in 1843:

Thus everything in economics stands on its head. Value, the primary factor, the source of price, is made dependent on price, its own product. As is well known, this inversion is the essence of abstraction; on which see Feuerbach (CW 3.427).

And in the 'Condition of England. The Eighteenth Century', written in early 1844, Engels commented:

Bentham here [in his utilitarian 'greatest happiness' principle] makes the same error in his empiricism as Hegel made in his theory; he does not seriously try to overcome the contradictions, he turns the subject into the predicate, subordinates the whole to the part and in so doing stands everything on its head (CW 3.486).

Evidently the inversion metaphor was intended to cover a multitude of sins characteristically though not exclusively practised by idealists; those sins were specified to some degree in Engels's early works. But in his 1859 criticisms Engels was so vague about the real relation involved that the metaphor is meaningless and the point of the criticism obscure. He was probably referring to the 'real relation' between 'being' and 'consciousness' that he had quoted from Marx's 1859 Preface. But though Engels perhaps took the non-inverted relationship to be the determination (in a sense unspecified by Engels *or* Marx) of 'consciousness' by 'social being', he also took the latter to be material in itself and dichotomously opposed to consciousness (SW 1.368, 372).

Within the 1859 review Engels sometimes seems to have meant by 'materialist conception' a view that social production is crucial when men (who are both conscious *and* material) make their own history. This was a view developed most notably in *The German Ideology* and always maintained by Marx. But Engels also referred in the 1859 review to the materialist conception as one in which 'it is demonstrated in each particular case how every time the action originated from direct material impulses and not from the phrases that accompanied the action' (SW 1.369). This was a marked departure from both his own previous ideas, and Marx's.

Quite what 'material' was intended to mean in this new context is far from clear, but the juxtaposition of 'material impulses' with 'the phrases that accompanied the action' suggests something rather more like the matter – consciousness dichotomy generally employed by natural scientists than the thesis in *The German Ideology* that 'consciousness can never be anything else than conscious being, and the being of men is their actual life-process'. In *The German Ideology* the matter – consciousness dichotomy was itself presented as ideological, in so far as an idealist realm of consciousness (a 'heaven') independent of men's real lives was postulated (CW 5.36).

While Engels certainly rejected idealism, his works after 1859 were *ambiguous* because of his failure to define precisely the 'materialist' nature of the 'materialist conception of history'. He employed the matter – consciousness dichotomy as found in contemporary natural science (which distinguished between the two as different, or apparently different types of phenomena) *and* the 'new' materialism of *The German Ideology*, which related events and ideas to man's productive development. In his 'new' materialism Marx did not take up a position on the matter – consciousness dichotomy, since what was important for him was the *relationship* between social being and consciousness, not their ultimate constituents, material or otherwise. In any case social being and consciousness were never defined dichotomously by Marx, since social being did not exclude ideas (used in practice), and consciousness (i.e. mere ideas) did not exclude a connection sooner or later with practical activities.

Contrary to Marx's discretion, Engels introduced an ontological issue into his account of the new outlook that was not a problem in *The German Ideology* nor in Marx's other works, namely the implications of the matter – consciousness debate for the study of history and contemporary society. In what way could political 'action' be linked to 'material impulses' which are, following the matter – consciousness dichotomy, exclusive of 'phrases' or 'consciousness' or 'ideas'? Engels never resolved this problem in his successive accounts, begun in 1859, of 'the basic materialist outlook'.

Marx's 'new' materialism, as he identified it in the *Theses on Feuerbach*, had in fact sidestepped the matter – consciousness dichotomy by making it irrelevant to his theories of society and social change. In opposition to 'all previous materialism' which accepted a matter – consciousness dichotomy, Marx founded his first proposition on 'the mode of production of material life', i.e. what *men* do in 'social production' (CW 5.3; SW 1.362–3). Significantly, in explicating Marx's more specific view of the role of the 'mode of production of material life' within 'social being' itself, Engels dropped the term 'mode of production' and substituted 'material conditions of life' as the basis from which 'epochs are understood', and then 'all the social and political relations, all religious and legal systems, all the theoretical outlooks which emerge in history' are 'comprehended' (SW 1.368). This marks a halfway point in the (apparently unconscious) transformation of Marx's man-centred formulations ('social being', 'mode of production') into Engels's obscurely 'materialist' account in which 'phrases' accompany 'the action' which originates from 'direct material impulses'. All these terms remained sublimely undefined in Engels's work, and it seems that he was unware of the problems intrinsic to concepts such as 'material impulses' and 'action', and by the relationship between his new terms and Marx's. By implying that the matter – consciousness dichotomy *was* relevant in interpreting Marx's concept of social being as materialist, Engels unnecessarily identified Marx's theories with a view in natural science that material and conscious phenomena are, or merely appear to be, ultimately distinct, and did nothing to clarify the ontological relationship between the two categories, save to reject an idealist view that matter is in some sense an emanation of consciousness.

The 'materialist outlook' itself was in any case subordinated by Engels to 'the method which forms the foundation of Marx's criticism of political economy'. This emerged, in Engels's account, as the 'logical method', and it, like the 'materialist outlook', also derived from Hegel's 'magnificent conception of history': Hegel's 'epoch-making conception of history was the direct theoretical premise for the new materialist outlook, and this alone provided a connecting point for the logical method, too'. The 'logical method' arose from Engels's consideration of the relationship between Hegel's 'thoughts' and the 'development of world history'. Hegel had used history, so Engels claimed, as the test of his philosophy by showing 'a development, an inner coherence, in history'. Engels praised this method very highly in the 1859 text, while implying that the 'inner coherence' identified by Hegel could not be the correct one, because his idealist view that history was the realisation of an *idea*, namely freedom, was in Engels's opinion quite erroneous. The logical method, however, was 'simple' and was, after some nugatory discussion, 'nothing else but the historical method, only divested of its historical form and disturbing fortuities'. That method was applied by Marx to the 'criticism of economics', but was not by any means limited to such a project, in Engels's view, since it was, after all, 'the only true form of development of thought' (SW 1.372–3).

How then were 'disturbing fortuities' to be sorted out from the 'historical course' of economic development in 'abstract and theoretically consistent form'? According to Engels, a reflection was 'corrected according to laws furnished by the real course of history itself'. He explained that the corrected reflection revealed 'each factor' in historical succession at 'the point of development of its full maturity, of its classic form'. But that account linking mature factors together was to be obtained by using 'laws' which were nowhere defined in the 1859 text. And no laws were mentioned by Marx in his 1859 Preface (SW 1.373–4).

In support of his view Engels made two sweeping claims about history and political economy: 1) 'in history... development as a whole proceeds from the most simple to the more complex relations', and 2) the 'literary reflection' of history, including 'the historical development of the literature of political economy', also develops 'from the most simple to the more complex relations' (SW 1.373).

For neither of those claims was any evidence offered by Engels. The alleged facts in his two points, however, were the ones which were supposed to form the test (as in Engels's view of Hegel's method) that in a logical development of concepts (in this case the 'economic categories') it is 'the *actual* development that is followed'. In that way Engels thought he had justified the presentation of 'the economic categories as a whole... in the same sequence as in the logical development' (SW 1.373–4).

It is possible that in formulating this argument Engels had in mind certain passages from the 'general introduction' which Marx told his readers had been scrapped in favour of the 1859 Preface to *A Contribution to the Critique of Political Economy* (SW 1.361). In his posthumously published 'general introduction' of 1857 Marx commented:

The economies of the seventeenth century, for example, always began with the living whole, the population, the nation, the state, more

states etc.; they always end, however, in such a way that they
discover a few determining, abstract, universal relationships, like
division of labour, money, value etc., through analysis. As soon as
those individual moments were more or less fixed and abstracted, the
economic systems which ascend from the simple [moment], such as
labour, division of labour, need [and] exchange-value, up to the state,
exchange among nations and the world market, began [to be
formulated]. The latter is obviously the scientifically correct method
(Carver (1975), 72).

While we do not know whether Engels actually read this text,
or had parts of it communicated to him verbally while Marx
was at work, there is no reason to rule this out. But when
Engels fastened on his 'logical method' as scientifically correct
because it embodied a *historical* sequence from simple categories to complex ones (as mentioned in Marx's 1857 'general
introduction'), he did so in defiance of the conclusion to that
discussion.

In the 'general introduction' Marx explored his initial view
on scientific method very thoroughly: 'However, do these
simple categories not have an independent historical or
natural existence before the more concrete categories? That
depends.' His crucial example was 'labour', which 'appears to
be a quite simple category'. Also, Marx continued, 'the
conception of it in that universality – as labour generally – is
very old'. Nevertheless, he concluded, labour is 'a modern
category in the same way as the relations which produce that
simple abstraction' (Carver (1975), 74, 76). From his investigation of 'labour' Marx generalised as follows:

That example of labour shows strikingly how the most abstract
categories themselves are, in the determinateness of that abstraction
itself – in spite of their validity for all epochs – their validity just on
account of being abstractions – just as much the product of historical
relations, and how they possess their full validity only for and within
those relations (Carver (1975), 78).

And about the implications for his own critical work on
political economy Marx was unequivocal:

Therefore it would be impracticable and false to let the economic
categories succeed one another in the sequence in which they were the

determining categories historically. Rather, their order of succession is determined by the relationship which they have to one another in modern bourgeois society, and that relationship is exactly the reverse of that which appears as their succession in accordance with nature or that which corresponds to the order of their historical development. We are not dealing with the relation [to each other] which the economic relations take up in the sequence of different forms of society... Rather [we are dealing] with their arrangement within modern bourgeois society (Carver (1975), 81).

Marx did not hold the view that the development of an economic category was necessarily a progression from simplicity to complexity, nor did he think that historical progression of categories (whether according to their first appearance or their importance in successive economic systems) was the proper model for his theoretical presentation. Rather he proposed to examine the economic categories which 'constitute the inner arrangement of bourgeois society', according to a plan which identified capital as 'the economic power of bourgeois society, the power ruling over everything'. For that reason, he argued, 'it must form the starting point'. And to explain capital, he began with the commodity and money (Carver (1975), 81–2, 134–6, 151–3).

While Marx observed a certain correspondence between logical and historical development, this was very much a subordinate point to the main argument rather than his organising principle. In his view there was never any possibility that the sequence commodity – money – capital could have appeared historically in some other order, since another order would be logically impossible. How could capital *be* what it is in a society without money, or money *be* money in a society without commodity production? Marx's starting point in his critique of political economy was never identified with the presumed historical origins of capitalist society, and he only occasionally amplified his abstract 'arrangement' of the *elements* of capitalist society with historical asides (see, for example, CCPE 50–1).

When Engels wrote that the 'chain of thought must begin with the same thing with which this history begins', he ran directly counter to Marx. And he misconstrued Marx's abstract arrangement of the essential elements of 'the economic conditions of life [in] . . . modern bourgeois society', because of his unwarranted assumption that historical development and 'literary reflection' advance from the most simple to the more complex relations. In fact Marx advised his readers in the 1859 Preface to 'be resolved to ascend from the particular to the general' as he moved from the commodity to money to capital (SW 1.361, 373).

Proceeding then from what he took to be the 'first and simplest' relation in history, Engels discerned a dialectical method in Marx's work: 'In this method we proceed from the first and simplest relation that historically and in fact confronts us; here, therefore, from the first economic relation to be found. We analyse this relation.' The recommended method was extraordinarily abstract and wholly without justification even as an *a priori* model for analysis: 'Being a *relation* of itself implies that it has two sides, *related to each other*. Each of these sides is considered by itself, which brings us to the way in which they behave to each other, their interaction. Contradictions will result which demand a solution.' Engels then announced that this was not 'an abstract process of thought taking place solely in our heads'; but, so he claimed, a 'real process which actually took place at some particular time or is still taking place'. These 'contradictions', he said, 'will have developed in practice and will probably have found their solution'. Even the form in which contradictions are resolved was specified in advance: 'We shall trace the nature of this solution, and shall discover that it has been brought about by the establishment of a new relation whose two opposite sides we shall now have to develop, and so on.' (SW 1.374).

Engels then praised Marx's presentation of the commodity not merely as a successful result of the dialectical method he had just outlined but as the correct solution to certain problems posed in political economy itself:

If now we consider commodities from their various aspects, commodities, to be sure, in their complete development and not as they first laboriously developed in the primitive barter between two primitive communities, they present themselves to us from the two points of view of use-value and exchange-value, and here we at once enter the sphere of economic dispute (SW 1.374).

While we might go on to agree with Engels that Marx's treatment of the commodity was 'as superior to the old, shallow, garrulous metaphysical method [of Adam Smith and others] as the railway is to the means of transport of the Middle Ages', it is difficult to see that Marx's procedure was successfully epitomised in Engels's schematic account, in which a commodity was said to be a *relation* which was then assumed to have two sides (use-value and exchange-value) which interact, producing contradiction and solution (the commodity as 'immediate unity of both') (SW 1.375). Marx's initial move in his 1859 *A Contribution to the Critique of Political Economy*, as in *Capital*, was to consider the 'wealth of bourgeois society', a particular 'unit' of which was the 'commodity'. He then clearly identified a commodity as a 'thing' and an 'object'. For Marx commodities were, of course, objects to which people *have* a relation; a commodity is an object 'of human wants, a means of existence . . .' (CCPE 27).

Engels confused the purposely abstract character of Marx's presentation by introducing an irrelevant distinction between producer and consumer of commodities at this early stage of explication. The distinction was not present at all in Marx's opening chapter, because any given person might be both or either with respect to the commodity as a value-in-exchange, though not of course to any particular commodity at any one time. Otherwise, on Marx's definition, the object in question would not *be* a commodity. Inaccurately, then, Engels described something as a commodity when 'a *relation* between two persons or communities attaches to the *thing*, the product, the relation between producer and consumer who are no longer united in the same person'. But for Marx mere disjuncture between producer and consumer was not the sufficient condition for commodity-exchange. Engels concluded, sweepingly, that 'economics deals not with things but with relations between persons'. He added moreover that those 'relations are . . . always *attached to things* and *appear as things*', but he did not explain how exactly a relation may be 'attached' to a thing or 'appear' as a thing (SW 1.374).

Marx's careful analysis, which began with things and the relations in which people stand to them, has a clarity that quite escaped Engels. This makes it difficult to conclude with Engels that it was the propositions about history, political economy and commodities that he had outlined in the 1859 review that enabled Marx to make 'the most difficult questions so simple and clear that now even the bourgeois economists will be able to grasp them' (SW 1.374). If Marx had in any sense accomplished that, it was not for the reasons given by Engels.

In his closing paragraph Engels returned to his theme that the theoretical and historical aspects of Marx's criticism of political economy proceeded in 'constant contact', something which was not true of Marx's account of the commodity in *A Contribution to the Critique of Political Economy*, even taken in conjunction with the 'Historical Notes on the Analysis of Commodities' in which he gave an overt, critical treatment of the history of political economy, later dropped from the main text and squeezed into the footnotes of volume one of *Capital*. Engels's apparatus of historical and literary development was simply an inaccurate reflection of the true state of affairs in history, the literature of political economy and Marx's critique. His 'dialectical' method – imputing an ontology of relations, and a specific methodology of 'sides', 'interaction', 'contradiction' and 'solution' to Marx – was erroneous in its presuppositions about the plan of Marx's presentation and unhelpful in its formulation of an overly abstract and allegedly universal procedure (SW 1.374–5).

Engels's preoccupation with method – following a prescribed sequence, finding short-cuts, ordering knowledge and experience – was foreign to Marx. Marx's own methodological claims were profoundly modest, and the methods he employed in solving problems, even when characterised by him (very rarely) as dialectical, were irreducible to propositions and procedures of the sort offered by Engels.

Marx's actual method in dealing critically with political economy was eclectic and very complex. He used classical and Hegelian logic, and the techniques of mathematical, sociological, economic, historical and political analysis. These came into play when they were appropriate to the matter at hand. This eclectic method included a notion of dialectic as the specification of conflictual, development factors in analysing social phenomena, and we know that Marx found this helpful in dealing, for example, with the concepts of money and profit (see Carver (1976), 60–8). But neither 'dialectic' nor any other methodological formula represents a 'master-key' to Marx's work. He rightly denied that such master-keys were of any use to anyone when he wrote this letter in November 1877. In it he confirmed the rejection of a Hegelian-style 'philosophy of history' previously rejected in *The German Ideology* and implicitly rejected in earlier works:

> Thus events strikingly analogous but taking place in different historical surroundings led to totally different results. By studying each of these forms of evolution separately and then comparing them one can easily find the clue to this phenomenon, but one will never arrive there by using as one's master-key a general historico-philosophical theory, the supreme virtue of which consists in being super-historical (SC 313).

In particular, Engels's 1859 presentation of Marx's method failed to do justice to Marx's work, since Engels gave the reader the impression that Marx perceived idealism as inverted (without explaining what this means); that he ordered economic concepts from the simple to the complex as history (allegedly) dictates; and that he treated things and objects as relations in a ready-made dialectical fashion, i.e. sides, interaction, contradiction, solution.

When introducing Marx's critique of political economy Engels seemed to reminisce about the days of *The German Ideology* – the battles against idealism. But he adopted the Hegelian notion that science as *Wissenschaft*, including history, can be treated in its 'inner interconnection', and projected that encyclopedic preoccupation (erroneously) onto Marx. He further assumed (unnecessarily) that Marx's new materialism was predicated on the materialism of natural science, hence he attributed to Marx a social science which (ambiguously) did and did not presuppose the matter – consciousness dichotomy. Moreover to Marx he assigned (fictitiously) a plan and dialectical method which he never employed either explicitly or implicitly in his works. Significantly Marx was far more concerned to get on with the substance of his critical work on capitalist society than to explain his methodology, a project briefly mentioned in a letter to Engels of 16 January 1858 and never carried out.

In his apparent reminiscences about the crucial period of the 1840s – the 'self-clarification' arising out of *The German Ideology* of 1845–46 – Engels shifted the focus of this clarification from results to a re-engagement with the questions posed by Hegelian philosophers and with their philosophical answers. *The German Ideology* cut through those academic debates to the empirical establishment of premises for social science and political action that cannot reasonably be doubted. These premises were living individuals, their activities and the material surroundings in which activities, pre-eminently production, are carried on. From his point of view in 1859, Engels had not really denied those premises so much as re-opened the traditional debates with which the Young Hegelians, to Marx's fury, had been almost wholly preoccupied. From Engels's rehearsal of these philosophical debates emerged *his* materialism, which was close in many respects to being a simple reversal of philosophical idealism *and* a faithful reflection of the natural sciences as portrayed by positivists. Engels was seemingly unware (or had he forgotten?) that *The German Ideology* had, in a sense, transcended those philosophical questions and their various philosophical solutions for new premises and, more importantly, *new questions* concerning the past, present and future development of society, particularly 'legal relations' and 'forms of state'. These were mentioned by Marx, in a part of the 1859 Preface not quoted by Engels, as the very problems to which the 'guiding thread' was addressed (SW 1.362). Thus Marx's work was transmogrified in Engels's 1859 review into the academic philosophy that the self-clarification of *The German Ideology* had triumphantly superseded.

Within the interpretative framework of the 1859 review Engels elevated method to a level of importance far higher than it assumed in any of Marx's very sparing comments on the subject. And within his account of Marx's allegedly 'true' methodology Engels placed particular emphasis on a debt to Hegel. Marx acknowledged a debt to Hegel some years later, in order to reply intelligently to critics who had raised the issue themselves, but his specification of the 'rational dialectic' was much less high-flown (and far more intelligible) than Engels's 'true form of development of thought' (see Carver (1982), 45–9).

Engels's emphasis on method over substance and his focus on Hegel's work as the *sine qua non* for getting to grips with Marx had profound intellectual consequences. He misrepresented Marx's enterprises as Hegelian in scope, and he initiated the now commonplace but profoundly academic view that a study of Hegel is essential to an understanding of Marx and his methods. In that way he set the pattern for almost all treatments, academic and otherwise, of Marx's lifework. Moreover the imposition of the categories materialism, idealism, dialectic, interaction, contradiction and reflection on Marx's work has redefined it as Marxist rather than strictly Marxian. In August 1859 Friedrich Engels invented dialectics, the progenitor of unresolvable ambiguities within the Marxist tradition.

5 'Second Fiddle'?

Engels pursued his new vocation – presenting Marx's ideas to the public – in works published anonymously or under his own name. These commentaries on Marx did not appear with an explicit imprimatur. Because of the discrepancies we perceive today between the material in Engels's commentaries and the texts Marx has left, the Marx–Engels relationship has become problematic to us, whether or not it was to them.

The actual relationship, so far as we know, continued in a relatively unruffled fashion until Marx's death on 14 March 1883. From that time onwards Engels became the custodian not only of Marx's works but of the relationship itself. The character of that relationship then became crucial for Engels, because in his hands it was made to validate his own presentation of Marx's ideas, which by then had acquired considerable political significance in Germany, France, Russia and other countries besides.

Thus for the period before Marx's death we are left wondering how he perceived Engels and his works, what he meant when he said the few informative things that he did about them, and to what extent, if any, his own outlook became influenced by Engels's distinctive point of view. Then for the period after Marx's death we must give careful consideration to Engels's version of their relationship and indeed to accounts of that relationship which draw their evidence from Engels; we must scrutinise any changes that occur in Engels's thought, particularly changes that might bear on our interpretation of his earlier writings when Marx was alive and on the discrepancy between their theories; and we must consider further Engels's commentaries which set a Marxist interpretation on Marx that runs counter to the ideas that he himself put forward.

The work in which 'Marxism' began to reach the socialist public in really significant numbers was undoubtedly Engels's *Herr Eugen Dühring's Revolution in Science*, first published in a newspaper, pamphlets and volume-form, all in 1877–8, and generally known as *Anti-Dühring*. Three chapters were subsequently published in French as *Socialism, Utopian and Scientific* in 1880 and then in German in this form in 1883. The complete book was republished in a second edition in 1886 and a third in 1894. Two years earlier Engels wrote a special introduction for the English edition of *Socialism, Utopian and Scientific*, commenting: 'I am not aware that any other socialist work, not even our Communist Manifesto of 1848 or Marx's *Capital*, has been so often translated. In Germany it has had four editions of about 20,000 copies in all' (SW 2.94–5). For that reason alone – wide-circulation – *Anti-Dühring* would be worth careful examination. But as it happens the work also contains Engels's most comprehensive attempt to present Marx's ideas, so we ought to pay it careful attention to see how accurately he did this. There are yet further reasons for examining Engels's *Anti-Dühring*. In successive prefaces Engels gave rather different accounts of the relationship between his own work in *Anti-Dühring* and Marx's views, depending on whether the preface was written before or after Marx's death. Moreover in those prefaces we are given different impressions of Marx's attitude to Engels's text and to Engels himself, again according to whether the preface dates from before or after 1883.

Eugen von Dühring, an academic at the University of Berlin, came to Marx's attention shortly after the publication of *Capital*, when Engels (several times reviewer of the work) commented on Dühring's 'highly amusing' piece in a letter. The following day Marx replied that Dühring had 'obviously misunderstood various things', the 'drollest' of which was that he had confused Marx himself with Lorenz von Stein (1815–90), author of a *System of Political Science* and the recently published *Theory of Administration*, 'because I cultivate the dialectic and Stein unthinkingly runs together the most trivial things into wooden trichotomies with a few Hegelian category-reversals'. Marx pursued Dühring's works on philosophy and political economy for a time, gleefully informing Engels of their worthlessness, but eliciting little response (MEW 32.8,9,11–12).

Because Dühring was a student of both Hegelian philosophy and contemporary political economy he was for Marx a particularly interesting opponent. Moreover any publicity was better than none. In a letter to his friend Ludwig Kugelmann sent on 6 March 1868, Marx mentioned both aspects of Dühring's work and commented: 'He is trying in bad faith to saddle me with Ricardian stupidities. But never mind. I must be grateful to the man, since he is the first professional who has spoken at all' (MEW 32.539).

Dühring went on to publish his *Critical History of Political Economy and Socialism* in 1871 and a *Course in Political Economy* in 1873. In 1875 a second edition of his *Critical History* appeared, as well as his *Course in Philosophy as a Strictly Scientific World Outlook and Pattern for Life.* The influence of Dühring's work among German socialists was particularly deplored by one of their leaders, Wilhelm Liebknecht, who wrote to Engels several times in 1875, urging him to attack Dühring in the socialist newspaper *Volksstaat.* Engels does not seem to have thought the matter all that urgent.

Later, in 1892, Engels wrote in some detail about the political circumstances surrounding the *Anti-Dühring* project, informing his readers that 'about 1875' Dühring had 'suddenly and rather clamourously announced his conversion to socialism, and presented the German public not only with an elaborate socialist theory, but also with a complete practical plan for the reorganisation of society'. With no doubt some exaggeration Engels recorded that Dühring had formed a sect which threatened to split the newly united German Socialist Party (SPD), formed in 1875 from two groups, known as Eisenachers (after their founding conference held in 1869) and Lassalleans (after Ferdinand Lassalle (1825–64), Marx's political rival). 'The Socialist Party in Germany was fast becoming a power', Engels wrote, but 'to make it a power, the first condition was that the newly-conquered unity should not be imperilled' (SW 2.93).

Somewhat nearer to these events, in the Preface (dated 11 June 1878) to the first edition of *Anti-Dühring*, Engels painted much the same political scene, but mentioned a personal reluctance to get involved which was not so extensively dwelt on in his later, more positive account. 'The following work [*Anti-Dühring*] is by no means the fruit of any "inner urge"', Engels wrote, 'on the contrary'. He explained that 'friends in Germany repeatedly urged on me their desire that I should subject this new socialist theory [by Dühring, 'a reformer of socialism'] to a critical examination'. *They* thought this necessary, Engels related, and *they* were in a better position to judge. 'It was a year before I could make up my mind to neglect other work and get my teeth into this sour apple' (AD 9–10).

We know that an article in praise of Dühring arrived for Engels's editorial inspection on 16 May 1876 and on the 24th he wrote to Marx, expressing concern that Dühring had acquired a very vocal supporter within the socialist camp. The difficulty this caused – a genuine attack on Dühring would be taken as an attack on certain personalities within the party – was also a problem. In a 'rage' he asked Marx, 'whether it isn't about time to give our position *vis-à-vis* this gentleman careful consideration'? It appears that the impetus for *Anti-Dühring* came from Engels himself, *not* Marx, as accounts based on *selected* correspondence have stated. Unsurprisingly Marx replied to Engels in agreement: 'My view is that the "position *vis à-vis* this gentleman" can only be taken up by criticising Dühring without mercy' (MEW 34.12–13, 14).

On 28 May 1876 Engels wrote to Marx with news of his plan for attacking Dühring and his works. Dühring's *Course in Philosophy*, according to Engels, 'better exposes the weak aspects and foundations of the arguments introduced in the "Economy"', the work which might have seemed of most interest to socialists. Engels's plan was logical, however: Dühring's 'banality', he commented, was revealed 'in a simpler form than in the economic book', and Engels proposed to take both together.

Thus the structure of *Anti-Dühring* was largely dictated by the subjects covered (very superficially, according to Engels) by Dühring. 'Of real philosophy', Engels complained, 'formal logic, dialectics, metaphysics, etc., there is nothing; rather it is supposed to present a general theory of science in which 'nature, history, society, state, law, etc., are discussed in a supposed inner connection' (MEW 34.17).

In his first preface Engels confirmed that 'it was thus the nature of the object itself which forced the criticism to go into such detail as is entirely out of proportion to the scientific content... of Dühring's writings'. But there were for Engels two further excuses for an extended critical treatment of Dühring's work. One was the need to smash a syndrome of 'system-building' that was rife in Germany. 'Herr Dühring', he alleged, 'is one of the most characteristic types of this bumptious pseudo-science... drowning everything with its resounding – sublime nonsense... This is an infantile disease which... our workers with their remarkably healthy nature will undoubtedly overcome' (AD 10–11). And in 1892, for an English audience, Engels came perilously close to self-parody in condemning Dühring for producing just the sort of 'system' which Engels himself manufactured in order to refute Dühring's views:

As is well known, we Germans are of a terribly ponderous *Gründlichkeit*, radical profundity or profound radicality, whatever you may like to call it. Whenever anyone of us expounds what he considers a new doctrine, he has first to elaborate it into an all-comprising system. He has to prove that both the first principles of logic and the fundamental laws of the universe had existed from all eternity for no other purpose than to ultimately lead to this newly-discovered, crowning theory. And Dr Dühring, in this respect, was quite up to the national mark (SW 2.93–4).

The other excuse for writing such an extended criticism of Dühring was 'the opportunity', as Engels put it in 1878, 'of setting forth in a positive form my views on controversial issues which are today of quite general scientific or practical interest'. Though Engels denied that the work aimed at presenting an alternative system, 'yet it is to be hoped', he continued in an almost self-contradictory remark, 'that the reader will not fail to observe the connection inherent in the various views which I have advanced' (AD 10).

But in the later prefaces, written after Marx's death, Engels became more open about offering a systematic alternative to Dühring, *and* he identified what had been described as 'my views' as 'views held by Marx and myself'. In pursuing Dühring across his 'wide theoretical domain', Engels informed us that 'the polemic was transformed into a more or less connected exposition of the dialectical method and of the communist world outlook fought for by Marx and myself'. Moreover 'the mode of outlook expounded in this book was founded and developed', said Engels, 'in far greater measure by Marx, and only in an insignificant degree by myself'. For that exposition Engels remarked that he had covered 'a fairly comprehensive range of subjects', from 'the concepts of time and space to Bimetallism; from the eternity of matter and motion to the perishable nature of moral ideas; from Darwin's natural selection to the education of youth in a future society'. Engels claimed to have given Marx's 'views' on these subjects 'a more connected form' (AD 10, 13; SW 2.94).

It is certainly true that Marx's views on these varied subjects (when he had views at all) were not originally presented in a connected form; but it must be observed that when he did touch on the topics mentioned by Engels, his writing reveals a considerable discretion quite opposed to Engels's account of what he was doing in *Anti-Dühring*, why he was doing it, and who was responsible for the views he published. The record of Engels's *actual* interchanges with Marx supports the story put forward in Engels's first preface of 1878, rather than the more elaborately collaborative account offered after Marx's death.

During the summer of 1876 Engels had reported to Marx from Ramsgate on his progress on an anti-Dühring, ridiculing the academic's ideas about nature, but not mentioning his own dialectic approach:

Corresponding to the ever-thickening seaside torpor [my] reading was naturally Herr Dühring's natural philosophy of reality. I have never before met with anything so natural as that. The whole procedure is with natural things, since everything is taken to be natural that seems natural to Herr Dühring, whereby he always proceeds from 'axiomatic propositions', for what is natural needs no proof (MEW 34.27).

Apparently Marx made no comment on this, nor indeed on

Engels's project until 3 March 1877, when he reported someone else's reaction to the first instalments of *Anti-Dühring*, published earlier that year. According to Marx, the writer P.L. Lavrov (1823–1900) praised the work but said that 'one' [Marx adds 'i.e. he'] was not accustomed to such 'mildness' in Engels's polemical writings (MEW 34.34). However, Engels had evidently asked Marx to examine Dühring's work on political economy, because on 5 March Marx enclosed his 'Dühringiana' in a letter to Engels, voicing an enthusiastic critique, but no real respect for Dühring or his views:

It was impossible for me to read the wretch without hitting him over and over right on the head.

Now that I have familiarised myself with him (and the part from Ricardo on, which I have not yet read, must contain many pearls of great price), which called for great patience, I am, ever-ready with club in hand, capable in future of enjoying him peacefully. Having once worked oneself into the fellow, so that his method is weighed off, he is then, as it were, an amusing scribbler (MEW 34.36).

Engels replied that Marx's 'critical history' was 'more than I need to polish off the wretch completely in this area', and that his friend Lavrov 'will have no more complaint about mildness with the final word on the "Philosophy" and still less with the "Economy"'. Engels worked on the economic section of his *Anti-Dühring* from June to August 1877, acknowledging (in a private letter) Marx's help, and on 8 August Marx sent him some notes on François Quesnay's *Tableau économique* (1766), one of the works surveyed by Dühring (MEW 34.37, 63, 68–70).

After that, comment on the substance of *Anti-Dühring* ceased in the Marx–Engels correspondence. The material prepared for Engels by Marx was *not* published in full in the first edition (1878) of *Anti-Dühring* as a complete book. Only in the preface to the second edition (1886) did Engels acknowledge Marx's authorship of some of the economic material, and only in the third edition (1894) did he explain exactly why he had cut down the critique sent him by Marx. In his 1885 preface to the second edition Engels wrote that Marx's chapter 'unfortunately had to be shortened somewhat by me for purely external reasons', but in the 1894 preface he enlarged on this, saying that in certain sections of the manuscript 'the critique of Dühring's propositions was overshadowed by Marx's own developments regarding the history of economics'. Engels then explained that, 'wherever the thread of the argument makes this possible', he has now 'omitted passages which refer exclusively to Herr Dühring's writings', and published Marx's work on the political economists William Petty, Dudley North, John Locke, David Hume and Quesnay instead (AD 14, 20–1; MEW 20.623–6 n.1).

As time passed Marx loomed ever larger in Engels's conception of *Anti-Dühring*. It was only in the preface to the second edition (after Marx's death) that Engels claimed that he 'read the whole manuscript' to Marx 'before it was printed'. There is nothing in the Marx–Engels correspondence, in their works, or anywhere else to support this story. Nor is there an explanation why Marx should have had to *listen* to it being read aloud.

In the 1885 preface to *Anti-Dühring* Engels also wrote that his 'exposition' of the Marx–Engels 'world outlook' should not appear without Marx's 'knowledge'. This, Engels said, was 'understood' between them. He thus gave the reader the impression that Marx approved his work as an expression of 'their' outlook, while avoiding the statement that Marx *agreed* explicitly to any such thing (AD 13–14). There are *no* recorded responses or revisions by Marx to the substance of Engels's work. In fact Engels did not seem to have revealed publicly during Marx's lifetime that he had been helped on the book by Marx, and there seems to have been no move to put Marx's name on the book or to gain and publicise an imprimatur.

However, in the 1885 preface Engels claimed much more than that Marx had merely approved the manuscript. Engels argued that he had to counter Dühring's system with a positive alternative, not just negative criticism. But in his surviving correspondence with Marx, Engels did not make any grand claims about countering Dühring's system with 'dialectical method' and 'communist world outlook'. The account written *before* Marx's death showed much more limited objectives:

My plan is ready. First of all I shall deal with this trash in a purely objective and apparently serious way, and then the treatment will become more trenchant as the proofs of the nonsense on the one hand and of the platitudes on the other begin to pile up, until at last a regular hailstorm comes pouring down on him (SC 306).

In the 1885 preface to *Anti-Dühring*, however, Engels put Marx's name to the first premise of what we now recognise as dialectical materialism: 'Marx and I were pretty well the only people to rescue conscious dialectics from German idealist philosophy and apply it in the materialist conception of nature and history.' Engels argued that 'conscious dialectics' was manifested in *laws* of 'complete simplicity and universality' to be discovered in nature, history, and 'thought' by 'working with concepts', i.e. recapitulating and rewriting natural science, history, philosophy and mathematics. About the discovery of dialectical laws in history and 'thought' Engels said no more in the 1885 preface, preferring to concentrate on discovering the laws of dialectics in *nature* (AD 15–20).

Engels's results, other than those appearing in *Anti-Dühring*, were contained in the manuscript published after his death as the *Dialectics of Nature*. In fact he broke off work on that manuscript in order to write *Anti-Dühring*. The immediate impulse for Engels to take up a dialectical interpretation of natural science had been his highly critical reaction to the second edition of Ludwig Büchner's *Man and his Place in Nature in the Past, Present and Future. Or: Where did we come from? Who are we? Where are we going?* The plan for a critique dates from very early in 1873, and in a letter to Marx of 30 May he set down his 'dialectical ideas on the natural sciences' and asked for help:

In bed this morning the following dialectical ideas on the natural sciences came into my head:
The subject-matter of natural science – matter in motion, bodies. Bodies cannot be separated from motion, their forms and kinds can only be known through motion; of bodies out of motion, out of relation to other bodies, nothing can be asserted. Only in motion does a body reveal what it is. Natural science therefore knows bodies by considering them in their relation to one another, in motion. The knowledge of the different forms of motion is the knowledge of bodies. The investigation of these different forms of motion is therefore the chief subject of natural science... Seated as you are

there at the centre of the natural sciences you will be in the best position to judge if there is anything in it (SC 281–2).

Marx's seldom-quoted reply to this was friendly, brief and non-committal: 'Have just received your letter which has pleased me greatly. But I do not want to hazard an opinion before I've had time to think the matter over and to consult the "authorities"' (MEW 33.82). The 'authorities', so far as we know, did not seem to have been very impressed with Engels's insights, though Marx tried to break this to him gently. Carl Schorlemmer (a professor of chemistry at Manchester) remarked that he agreed that the 'investigation of these different forms of motion is therefore the chief subject of natural science' and that motion of a single body must be treated relatively ('Quite right!' he commented). But when Engels wrote that dialectics, as *the* scientific *Weltanschauung*, cannot itself advance from chemistry to 'organic science' until chemistry *itself* did so, and then (with respect to biology), 'Organism – here I will not enter into any dialectics for the time being', Schorlemmer commented 'Me neither' (MEW 33.80–1, 82–4). Marx's 'authority' found the science in Engels's letter more agreeable than the dialectics.

There is no more surviving correspondence between Marx and Engels concerning the *Dialectics of Nature* until Engels's letter of 21 September 1874, in which he related that articles by John Tyndall and T.H. Huxley in *Nature* have 'thrown me ... back onto the dialectical theme' (MEW 33.119–20). Again, there is no surviving comment from Marx, though on several occasions he referred to Engels's project in a respectful but distant way and even made brief formal inquiries for him. On 7 October 1876 he wrote to Wilhelm Liebknecht: 'Engels is busy with the Dühring work. It is a great sacrifice on his part since he has had to interrupt for this purpose a disproportionately more important work' (MEW 34.209). To Wilhelm Alexander Freund (a German gynaecologist) he addressed a query on 21 January 1877: 'If by chance you see Dr Traube [a German chemist and physiologist] ... remind him, if you please, that he has promised to send me the *titles* of his various publications. This would be very important for my friend Engels who is labouring on a work of natural philosophy and,

as it happens, Traube's achievements are emphasised'
(MEW 34.245–6). And to Wilhelm Blos (a German social-
democrat and journalist) he wrote on 10 November 1877:
'Generally my health forces me to forego labour-time per-
mitted me by the doctor for the completion of my work; and
Engels, who is working on various larger writings [*Dialectics of
Nature*] is still providing contributions [*Anti-Dühring et al.*] for
Vorwärts' (MEW 34.311).

There is no indication here that Marx identified himself with
either of Engels's works, or saw them as some aspect of their
joint 'outlook'. He was explicit in attributing these projects to
Engels and conspicuous in omitting to declare that they were in
any way a collaboration. In a later exchange on Engels's
research for the *Dialectics of Nature* Marx was almost crush-
ingly brief. On 23 November 1882 Engels wrote with a fanfare:

Electricity has afforded me no small triumph. Perhaps you recall my
discussion of the Descartes – Leibniz dispute... *Resistance* represents in electricity the same thing that *mass* does in mechanical
motion – here speed, there strength of current – the quantitatively
measurable form of appearance of that motion operates, in the case
of a simple transition *without* change of form, as a simple factor of the
first power; but in a transition *with* change of form, it operates as a
quadratic factor. This is a general natural law of motion which I have
formulated for the first time (MEW 35.118–19).

Marx's reply of 27 November (rarely cited) was stunningly
brief and non-committal, given the nature of the 'discovery':
'The confirmation of the role of the *quadratic* in the transition
of energy with a change of form of the latter is very nice, and I
congratulate you' (MEW 35.120). Evidently Marx did not rush
to any conclusions about natural laws, never mind dialectical
ones of the type unveiled by Engels.

The surviving Marx–Engels correspondence fails to support the picture painted by Engels in the 1885 preface to *Anti-
Dühring*. Marx did not discuss Engels's dialectical laws, even
after prodding, nor did he say anything to substantiate the
contention that he and Engels were joint expositors of a
universal materialism predicated on the natural sciences,
understood as the study of matter in motion. Marx said
nothing to confirm Engels's claim that he was familiar with the

lengthy text of *Anti-Dühring*, much less that he endorsed it in full.

Moreover the Marx–Engels correspondence does not corroborate the traditional account of their 'close collaboration' on all subjects, above all their theoretical work in what are alleged to be consistent and interchangeable writings. In fact, the correspondence strongly suggests that apart from political news, family gossip, and party affairs the two worked independently for the most part, and that requests for advice on fundamental theoretical points from either side produced very little of substance. The *Selected Correspondence*, be it noted, frequently omits *replies*. If highly significant interchanges had taken place between the two when they actually met, such letters as survive would surely reflect this, or at the very least they would not be so perfunctory and non-committal. The hypothesis that the two men had important theoretical discussions in private is not consistent with what they actually said in their letters. If there were evidence that would support the dialectical and materialist views propounded by Marx's literary executor (Engels), or if there were proof that their intellectual relationship was really as monolithic as Engels claimed after Marx's death, who in the Marx family or among their socialist colleagues would have had an interest in destroying it? If we examine both sides of any selection of correspondence and look beyond Engels's uncorroborated accounts, particularly ones that were written after Marx was in the grave, the traditional view (which derives from Engels's comments, for example in the prefaces to *Anti-Dühring*) simply crumbles away.

However, if Marx found himself seriously at odds with Engels over the substance of *Anti-Dühring*, why did he not dissociate himself from it? Or had he never read it (or listened to it) in the first place? *Anti-Dühring* appeared during 1877–78 in instalments, which Marx could easily have read, and it was also published as three pamphlets (1877–78) and as a book (1878). Even if Engels's story about reading the manuscript to Marx were untrue, or if Marx were not listening, it seems perverse to imagine that he ignored the content of the work altogether. Perhaps Marx felt it easier, in view of their long friendship, their role as leading socialists, and the usefulness of

Engels's financial resources, to keep quiet and not to interfere in Engels's work. After all, *Anti-Dühring* went out under Engels's name alone, Engels stated in the preface that the work contained 'my views', and neither Engels nor Marx seems to have revealed publicly during Marx's lifetime that Marx contributed to the chapter on political economy.

Interestingly Engels did not claim to have shown Marx the *Dialectics of Nature*, on which he started work in 1873. In those manuscripts his views on the general nature of dialectics were formulated explicitly, which was *not* the case in the *first* edition of *Anti-Dühring*. In this passage (written in 1879) from the manuscripts collected as the *Dialectics of Nature* (and post-humously published in full only in 1925), Engels summarised his outlook as a systematising philosophy based on the Hegelian model and explicitly derived from Hegel's work:

(The general nature of dialectics to be developed as the science of inter-connections, in contrast to metaphysics.)

It is, therefore, from the history of nature and human society that the laws of dialectics are abstracted. For they are nothing but the most general laws of these two aspects of historical development, as well as of thought itself. And indeed they can be reduced in the main to three:

The law of the transformation of quantity into quality and *vice versa*;

The law of the interpenetration of opposites;

The law of the negation of the negation.

All three are developed by Hegel in his idealist fashion as mere laws of *thought*: the first, in the first part of his *Logic*, in the Doctrine of Being; the second fills the whole of the second and by far the most important part of his *Logic*, the Doctrine of Essence; finally the third figures as the fundamental law for the construction of the whole system. The mistake lies in the fact that these laws are foisted on nature and history as laws of thought, and not deduced from them. This is the source of the whole forced and often outrageous treatment; the universe, willy-nilly, has to conform to a system of thought which itself is only the product of a definite stage of evolution of human thought. If we turn the thing round, then everything becomes simple, and the dialectical laws that look so extremely mysterious in idealist philosophy at once become simple and clear as noonday (DN 83–4).

The distillation of Engels's dialectics contained in the 1885 preface put the text of *Anti-Dühring* in a different light. Engels, it seems, was canny enough to avoid creating disagreements with Marx. And Marx seems to have been similarly canny in not pressing Engels on his work. In the first edition of Anti-Dühring dialectical laws appeared in the text, but without the ambitiously Hegelian advertisement that figured in the second preface:

It goes without saying that my recapitulation of mathematics and the natural sciences was undertaken in order to convince myself also in detail – of what in general I was not in doubt – that in nature, amid the welter of innumerable changes, the same dialectical laws of motion force their way through as those which in history govern the apparent fortuitousness of events; the same laws as those which similarly form the thread running through the history of the development of human thought and gradually rise to consciousness in the mind of man; the laws which Hegel first developed in all-embracing but mystic form, and which we made it one of our aims to strip of this mystic form and to bring clearly before the mind in their complete simplicity and universality (AD 16).

It was possible for Marx to take the view that the first edition of *Anti-Dühring* would do more good than harm, since he detested Dühring's views and Engels picked on them without mercy. Marx also recommended the book to others, referring almost gnomically to Engels's 'positive developments' and to the political importance of *Anti-Dühring* for 'a correct assessment of German socialism', without committing himself to every implication of the text or to the view that it could be read instead of *Capital*. This was a notion that Engels encouraged in private, particularly when he published a few chapters as *Socialism, Utopian and Scientific* in 1880 (MEW 34.263–4, 346). Least of all did Marx commit himself to Engels's later glosses on *Anti-Dühring* or to what Engels subsequently claimed about the relationship between their separate works and indeed between the two men themselves in their authorial roles. In a letter to his socialist friend F.A. Sorge written in late 1882, Engels drew an explicit comparison between his own little book and the opening volume of Marx's masterpiece *Capital* that was not wholly to the advantage of the latter; Engels even suggested that *Socialism, Utopian and Scientific* might safely substitute for the longer text:

You know, [Paul] Lafargue [French socialist and Marx's son-in-law]... has translated into French three chapters of my *Anti-Dühring*... under the title *Socialism, Utopian and Scientific*. The effect in France was enormous. Most people are too idle to read thick books like *Capital*, and so a little pamphlet does the job much more quickly (MEW 35.396).

Marx's rather distant preface to Engels's pamphlet was published as the work of Paul Lafargue. This may have been a tactical move to improve circulation of the work, but it may also have been an easy way for Marx to maintain his distance. Had the Marx–Engels partnership functioned in the intimate way described by Engels, Marx would surely have put his name to the one document in which he actually addressed himself (albeit with a certain vagueness) to Engels's theoretical efforts (MEW 19.181–2, 564 n. 113).

In the 1885 preface to *Anti-Dühring* Engels made it easy for his readers to conclude that within the Marx–Engels relationship the natural sciences were left to the latter; Engels wrote that 'a knowledge of mathematics and natural science is essential to a conception of nature which is dialectical and at the same time materialist. Marx was well versed in mathematics' (AD 15). Did Marx in fact leave natural science to Engels? Did he simply omit to do for the natural sciences what he had started to do for political economy and planned to do for law, morals, politics etc.? Or was natural science relevant to his work only in so far as it figured in his critical approach to modern capitalist society?

It is evident from his works that Marx had a serious interest in the natural sciences, though one subordinate (like everything else) to his critique of political economy. There is no support then for the suggestion that the natural sciences were left to Engels or that they required in Marx's view a 'critique' of the sort offered by his friend in order to square them with his own conception of society and social change. Moreover Marx neither endorsed nor made any claims about nature, history and 'thought' in his surviving letters or works that remotely resembled Engels's enthusiastic speculations on the power of dialectics to comprehend 'things and their representations, in their essential connection, concatenation, motion, origin and ending' (AD 33).

One of the best known comments by Marx on the natural sciences occurs in *Capital*, when he writes that the molecular theory in chemistry (as expressed in a series of homologous compounds) illustrates Hegel's analysis of the transformation of quantity into quality. Here Marx cites *Hegel* (not 'dialectics') and molecular theory to back up his claim that the qualitative change from master craftsman to capitalist follows from the accumulation of commodities or money beyond a critical quantity (CAP 1.292). What Marx *never* did was to claim that there are dialectical laws of *matter* in motion forcing their way through these transformations, 'the great basic process', as Engels put it in the 1885 preface to *Anti-Dühring* (AD 19).

When Marx referred in *Capital* to a correspondence between Hegel's supposedly pure conceptual analysis and certain physical and social phenomena once they have been explained, he merely noted that Hegel's insight applies in certain instances. When Marx termed Hegel's conclusion a 'law', he indicated that in some circumstances we can expect quantitative accumulation to produce qualitative change. In making that remark in *Capital* Marx was endorsing neither a metaphysics of Hegelian laws nor the 'scientific' *Weltanschauung* of Engels. When Marx commented on a correspondence between a proposition in Hegelian logic and the theory of chemical change, the now controversial character of his words would not have been apparent, because Engels's view that one set of dialectical laws accounts for all phenomena was not explicitly published until after Marx's death.

Marx admired the methods of reputable physicists and chemists, but carefully drew limits around the analogy between his methods and those of physical scientists. In his Preface to volume one of *Capital* he drew a double analogy between his critique and the work of natural scientists, in particular biologists and other physical scientists such as physicists and chemists. The commodity, he suggested, was the 'economic cell-form' of bourgeois society, as real cells go to make up a larger organic body; as with biology, it had taken many centuries to 'get to the bottom' of such 'minutiae'. Furthermore, just as the physicist 'either observes physical phenomena where they occur in their most typical form and most free from disturbing influence, or, wherever possible, he makes experiments under conditions that assure the occurrence of the phenomenon in its normality', so Marx used England 'as the chief illustration in the development of my theoretical ideas', because there one found 'the classic ground' of the capitalist mode of production. But Marx also took the trouble to declare limitations to this analogy with science, when he announced that 'neither microscopes nor chemical reagents are of use' in his work, since a quite different method, 'the force of abstraction', was appropriate. Science-worship was never part of Marx's theoretical apparatus (CAP 1.19).

Though Marx asserted the existence of material reality as a presupposition for his theory, he never presented his results as in any way derived from or based on laws of matter in motion. Engels's 'progress', during his career, from productively active individuals to molecular motion was, so far as we know, *never* endorsed by Marx. Of course *physical* consciousness has something to do with molecular motion, but there is no reason to suppose that Marx (whose interest was, anyway, in *social* consciousness) was any more convinced than scientists are today by Engels's 'proof' that dialectical laws of motion must underlie any satisfactory theory in psychology, history and other natural and social sciences. Engels might be right, but he has not made his case.

What Marx had to say about mathematics, physics, chemistry, biology, anthropology or logic does not disturb this picture. He pursued all these subjects with vigour when they were relevant to his work, contrary to the fiction that he and Engels participated in a conscious or unconscious division of labour. In such comments as he made on science, even to Engels himself, Marx never endorsed the materialist dialectics we now know that Engels was pursuing.

The scientific character of materialist dialectics was later defended by Engels in relation to 'three great discoveries which have enabled our knowledge of the interconnection of natural processes to advance by leaps and bounds'. The first was the 'discovery of the cell' which, according to Engels, led to the recognition that 'the development and growth of all higher organisms' proceeds 'according to a single general law'. Marx's own comments on the cell-form (quoted above) were much more guarded and were focussed in particular on the (limited) relevance of this discovery to the matter in hand – making his critique of political economy comprehensible to his readers. Engels's second example, 'the transformation of energy' as a law of 'universal motion', was mentioned to Marx in correspondence which has been discussed above, and Marx's reticence has been noted. The third was Darwin's work, which Engels took to be a 'proof' that the 'stock of organic products', including man, 'is the result of a long process of evolution from a few originally unicellular germs . . . which came into existence by chemical means' (SW 610, 611).

The Marx–Darwin relationship has been obscured by misinterpretations of what Marx actually said about him, by what is now known to be a false view of their personal relationship, and by a willingness of commentators to accept at face value what Engels said about the views of Marx and Darwin and the relationship between them. While Marx was amused that Darwin's presentation of the natural world unconsciously mimicked 'his English society with its division of labour, competition, opening of new markets, "inventions" and the Malthusian "struggle for existence"', he never disputed Darwin's presentation of the facts, and even described *The Origin of Species* 'as a natural-scientific basis' for his own views (SC 123, 128). Marx, Engels and Darwin were all thoroughly sceptical about any attempt to employ natural selection, i.e. survival and reproductive advantage, to human life and history. For Marx and Engels, class struggle (not the mere survival of 'fit' individuals) was the most important category in social analysis, though on the presuppositions of that analysis Marx's 'new' materialism and Engels's ambiguous 'materialist interpretation of history' were rather different. Engels's notion of historical progress (examined below) resembled the evolutionism espoused by Social Darwinists, though not by Darwin himself, and certainly not by Marx.

While it is true that Marx sent Darwin an inscribed copy of the first volume of *Capital* (in the second German edition) in 1873, he did the same for others. A new analysis of surviving correspondence from Darwin now suggests that there is no convincing reason to believe that Marx intended to dedicate any part, edition or translation of *Capital* (or any other work) to Darwin, who was, it seems, approached by Marx's son-in-law Edward Aveling concerning a dedication to a book that he, not Marx, was writing. While Engels was sceptical of a Darwinist approach to human history in general (though admitting a similarity between Darwin's struggle and a *bellum omnium contra omnes* in *bourgeois* society specifically), he attributed to Marx and Darwin a common methodology coincident with his own positivist view of science. 'Just as Darwin discovered the law of development of organic nature', Engels announced in his speech at Marx's graveside, 'so Marx discovered the law of development of human history' (SC 171–3; SW 429). Both Marx and Darwin proposed general theories, one on the development of human society through changes in productive activities, the other on the origin of new species through variability, inheritance and natural selection. Yet neither generalisation has the same function as the mathematical 'laws of motion' established in chemistry and physics, to which Engels turned as models for scientific practice. Engels's enthusiasm for a unified view of science led him to a very hasty attribution of law-like truth to what were in fact useful hypotheses for guiding research in biology and social science respectively (see Carver (1982), 36, 55, 62, 66).

Since Engels's model of science was inductive (the 'facts' provide the 'view'), causal and law-directed, his projection of those presuppositions onto Marx's work has caused difficulties (SW 610–11). This happens when commentators have attempted to square Engels's view of what Marx's work *should* be like with what in fact it says. Neither Marx's correspondence nor the comments on the social and natural sciences in his works support the 'scientific' *Weltanschauung* propounded by Engels after Marx's death and elaborated in Engels's posthumously published manuscripts. Laws of dialectics do not appear in Marx's Preface to *A Contribution to the Critique of Political Economy* of 1859, his popular work *Wages, Price and Profit*, his masterpiece *Capital* and associated manuscripts, nor in his last work of theoretical interest, the *Notes on Adolph Wagner* (a German political economist). What Marx actually said about social science and natural science in these works does not bear at all on Engels's grandiose claims about matter in motion and dialectical laws. And the diffidence, lacunae and artful evasion displayed in Marx's replies to Engels does not illustrate a perfect partnership on theoretical issues. Engels presented his 'dialectical' views on 'thought' and history in various works published after Marx's death. In *Ludwig Feuerbach and the End of Classical German Philosophy*, which was primarily devoted to 'thought' (an ambiguous catch-all for philosophy and correct logical thinking), Engels also undertook an account of his own career and partnership with Marx. 'History' was Engels's again ambiguous catch-all for recent events and those (specifiable or in some cases purely speculative) of the distant past. On this subject Engels continued his own substantial work in *The Origin of the Family, Private Property and the State*, and his views on history were further rehearsed in numerous introductions to Marx's works. In that way the claimed connection between his 'dialectical' version of their 'outlook' and Marx's own ideas was intentionally reinforced. Those introductions represent an important but little-used source for a final assessment of the Marx–Engels intellectual relationship.

In 1886 Engels reviewed K.N. Starcke's *Ludwig Feuerbach* at length in a work entitled *Ludwig Feuerbach and the End of Classical German Philosophy*, which was published two years later in book form. His task was undertaken willingly, he said, because 'a short, coherent account of *our* relation to the Hegelian philosophy, of how *we* proceeded, as well as of how *we* separated, from it [my emphasis]' was required to clarify 'the Marxist world outlook'. 'We have expressed ourselves in various places', he continued, 'but nowhere in a comprehensive, connected account', something that Marx, on Engels's presumption, would have undertaken if he had had more time (SW 584–5). We have no evidence that Marx's early interest in presenting Hegel's achievements in relation to his own work on political economy would ever have coincided with Engels's 'materialist' philosophy as expounded in his long review.

In fact Engels downgraded what he possessed of *The German Ideology*, the work in which Marx achieved 'self-clarification' while disposing of Young Hegelianism. Engels wrote that the section on Feuerbach 'contains no criticism of Feuerbach's doctrine itself' and 'for the present purpose' was therefore unusable. The 'self-clarification' achieved in 1845–46 proved, according to Engels's view some forty years later, 'only how incomplete our knowledge of economic history still was at that time' (SW 585).

Ludwig Feuerbach and the End of Classical German Philosophy reproduced Engels's 1859 framework for interpreting Marx's lifework. His focus was on Marx's method (ambiguously logical and historical as before), its relation to Hegel's 'dialectical method' (in a textually controversial account), and the philosophically comprehensive character (according to Engels) of Marx's enterprise. The empirical content of Marx's early work and its thrust towards the 'social question' – his focus on poverty, wealth, and property in general – went unmentioned, as opposed to the emphasis they received in Marx's own 1859 autobiographical sketch. Even though the *Rheinische Zeitung*, in Engels's view, 'used the meagre cloak of philosophy only to deceive the censorship', he identified the paper with 'the *philosophy* of the aspiring radical bourgeoisie [my emphasis]', an incongruously academic note, given Marx's fiercely political stance. Marx had promoted his views, perhaps through tactical and intellectual necessity, in an ultra-academic style, so it is possible that Engels somewhat missed the point, at least in retrospect. While noting that Marx had had (unspecified) 'critical reservations' about Feuerbach's work, Engels then declared, 'we all at once became Feuerbachians'. This was surely an exaggeration in Marx's case, since his interests, projects and ambitions as a revolutionary were in practice quite unlike those of the famous philosopher. Feuerbach, in Engels's view, was unable to make use of 'the encyclopedic wealth of the Hegelian system' to which Marx was the rightful heir. 'It was resolved', Engels wrote, 'to comprehend the real world – nature and history'. In the 'tendency ... essentially connected with the name of Marx', the materialistic world outlook 'was carried through consistently – at least in its basic features – in all domains of knowledge concerned' (SW 591–2, 608). Engels thus voiced his dissatisfaction with the (in his view) insufficiently thorough attention paid in the 1840s to the construction of a materialism to surmount Hegel's comprehensive treatment of logic, history and nature.

Engels constructed a metaphysics for Marx (i.e. a view of ultimate causes and fundamental processes in the universe), though he did not label it as such, because of his identification of metaphysics with a belief in fixed referents for all concepts and with undialectical thinking (according to his view of dialectic). 'The great basic thought', Engels wrote, was 'that the world is not to be comprehended' (*comprehension* was his aim, as in the 1859 review) 'as a complex of ready-made *things*, but as a complex of *processes*'. Hegelian philosophy was not a necessary prolegomenon to the discovery of this truth; Engels remarked that Joseph Dietzgen (1828–88), 'a German worker' (and entrepreneurial philosopher) had also come to this conclusion and popularised it in his *The Nature of Human Brainwork* (1869). Engels then defined concepts (somewhat simply) as 'mind images' of 'things'; both 'go through an uninterrupted change of coming into being and passing away'. Dialectical philosophy 'reveals the transitory character of everything and in everything; nothing can endure before it except the uninterrupted process of becoming and passing away' (SW 588, 608–9). When Marx described *his* dialectic he noted that it recognised the 'affirmative', 'negation' and 'inevitable breaking up' of 'the existing state of things', i.e. capitalist society – a rather more limited object of study than Engels's 'everything' (CAP 1.29).

Engels's metaphysics was not mere Heraclitean flux, however, but 'progressive', an 'endless ascendancy from the lower to the higher'. In spite of all seeming accidentality of... temporary retrogression', Engels wrote, 'a progressive development asserts itself in the end' (SW 588, 609). Marx was no stranger to the idea of progress in *human* history, noting (in his 1859 Preface) that 'in broad outlines' there have been four 'progressive epochs in the economic formation of society' (SW 182). But these do not seem to form a distinct series; rather they are three contrasts with the industrial progress of modern bourgeois society, on which point Marx had no doubts. In any case it was modern bourgeois society in which Marx was interested, not historical progress as such. His few remarks about such progress are not nearly enough to identify him with an evolutionary philosophy of history, in which all stages form (in some sense) progressive steps towards an ever-superior or even perfect outcome. Marx's views on communist society, however optimistically inchoate, were supported (so he claimed) by his baring of 'the economic law of motion of modern society', and on *that* basis proletarian revolution was held to be 'inevitable', as stated in both the Communist Manifesto and *Capital* (SW 46, 229).

Had Marx been inclined to rely on a 'super-historical' construct, such as Engels's *a priori* metaphysics, he need never have bothered with the critique of political economy, undertaken after his journalistic encounters with 'so-called material interests' and pursued till his death (SC 313; SW 180). A metaphysics was not merely omitted from his work for one contingent reason or another; his work ran quite counter to the notion that a metaphysics as such was indeed necessary at all.

'Dialectics', Engels concluded, was 'the science of the general laws of motion, both of the external world and of human thought – two sets of laws which are identical in substance, but differ in their expression in so far as the human mind can apply them consciously'. Here the dialectical outlook foundered on a difficulty Engels was incapable of resolving, or even perhaps of recognising in the first place. If the 'dialectic of concepts' is 'the conscious reflex of the dialectical motion of the real world' – nature and history, where 'these laws assert themselves unconsciously' – how is it that these laws, which could with sufficient sophistication be perceived by men, then be applied 'consciously'? Is the result of this application a reduction in the number of 'seeming accidents' through which 'external necessity' is asserting itself? No actual applications of these laws were ever cited by Engels in anything other than an academic and theoretical sense; the world was never shown to have approached the smooth realisation of necessity any more closely because a dialectical law had been consciously applied. Indeed necessity and progress were never themselves defined so that such cases could be discussed. Engels's 'laws' of 'thought' were never even the beginnings of a logic. They worked in a way which was almost the reverse of any formation of categories to made discriminations, merely asserting the existence of 'interconnections' which were never systematically defined nor even demonstrated (SW 609). In so far as they functioned as a metaphysics, they were factitious and never relevant to Marx's work.

Engels's summary of his dialectical views on history in *Ludwig Feuerbach and the End of Classical German Philosophy* reproduced the ambiguous materialism of the 1859 review, still unresolved. Was he taking man to be material in some minimal sense, but crucially active, in a conscious way, in and on the material environment? Or was he taking man in a more determinately material sense, i.e. subject to laws in his social behaviour in the same way that matter is presented as law-governed in natural science? Engels's presentation of 'the Marxist world-outlook' in his 1886 version was somewhat inclined to assertions that men are subject to the same dialectical laws as governed nature and 'thought', probably because his self-proclaimed task was the demonstration that the materialism he assigned to Marx was coincident with just that sort of systematic, 'scientific' account.

While admitting a difference between 'the realm of nature' and 'the history of society', because of the role of human consciousness in the latter, Engels noted that this distinction was important for the investigation of 'single epochs and events'. But it was also ultimately compatible with his view that, like nature, history 'is governed by inner general laws', the same laws, in fact. He linked his search for the 'real ultimate driving forces of history' to individual wills – 'passion or deliberation' – and those factors to only certain motives 'which set in motion great masses, whole peoples, and again whole classes . . . not momentarily . . . but for a lasting action resulting in a great historical transformation'. Thus in a virtually circular account of the 'driving forces' which generate class struggles, Engels reached the position of the Communist Manifesto – 'all political struggles are class struggles' – and then went on to his 1859 variant on Marx's Preface – the substitution of 'economic conditions' for 'mode of production', resulting in an ambiguously 'materialistic' account. Thus he looked for an 'explanation' of the state and public law 'in the last resort' by the 'economic conditions of life of society', rather than for a Marx-like *investigation* of social events, in which 'the mode of production of material life *conditions* the social, political and intellectual life process in general' [my emphasis]. Engels referred in *Ludwig Feuerbach and the End of Classical German Philosophy* to 'the material, economic basis', but left us wondering whether he realised at all that this juxtaposition of terms needed careful examination (SW 181, 611–17).

Before 1859 Engels's substantial works on historical subjects resembled Marx's in certain respects, but after 1859 his work shifted in a way that revealed the discrepancy between Marx's work and his. *Revolution and Counter-Revolution in Germany*, written between August 1851 and September 1852, was composed by Engels but published with Marx's signature, so Marx could establish himself as correspondent for the New York *Daily Tribune* (and gain time to get his English up to standard). The work is very much a counterpart, for Germany, to Marx's *Class Struggles in France*, written a few months earlier in German, and it dealt with much the same period, the revolutionary events of 1848–49.

Marx and Engels used a common analytic method – class analysis – and were set the same problem by the revolutions in both Germany and France: how to explain their defeat. Class analysis was used, very effectively, to probe the causes of defeat and to explore the interests and trends that would condition political activity, particularly of the revolutionary sort, in future:

Class Struggles (Marx)	*Revolution and Counter-Revolution* (Engels)
With the exception of only a few chapters, every more important part of the annals of the revolution from 1848 to 1849 carries the heading: *Defeat of the Revolution!*	The preceding short sketch of the most important of the classes, which in their aggregate formed the German nation at the outbreak of the recent movements, will already be sufficient to explain a great part of the incoherence, incongruence and apparent contradiction which prevailed in that movement. When interests so varied, so conflicting,
What succumbed in these defeats was not the revolution. It was the pre-revolutionary traditional appendages, results of social relationships which had not	

yet come to the point of sharp class antagonisms – persons, illusions, conceptions, projects from which the revolutionary party before the February Revolution was not free, from which it could be freed not by the *victory of February*, but only by a series of *defeats*. In a word the revolution made progress, forged ahead, not by its immediate tragi-comic achievements, but on the contrary by the creation of a powerful, united counter-revolution, by the creation of an opponent in combat with whom alone the party of insurrection ripened into a really revolutionary party (CW 10.47).

so strangely crossing each other, are brought into violent collision; when these contending interests in every district, every province are mixed in different proportions; when, above all, there is no great centre in the country, no London, no Paris, the decisions of which, by their weight, may supersede the necessity of fighting out the same quarrel over and over again in every single locality; what else is to be expected but that the contest will dissolve itself into a mass of unconnected struggles, in which an enormous quantity of blood, energy and capital is spent, but which for all that remain without any decisive results? (CW 11.12).

Engels's *The Peasant War in Germany* (of 1525) was written in mid-1850; it was frankly a work with a political message of current interest, since it presented German readers with a stirring account of the German 'revolutionary tradition': 'There was a time when Germany produced characters that could match the best men in the revolutions of other countries, when the German people displayed an endurance and vigour which would in a more centralised nation have yielded the most magnificent results'. In his own time, Engels contended, 'the opponents who have to be fought are still essentially the same' as in the sixteenth century, and those 'classes and fractions of classes' which betrayed the insurgents of 1848 played a similar dastardly role three centuries earlier (CW 10.399).

The class analysis and firm contemporary focus were both characteristic, in a general way, of Marx's work, even on historical subjects, though his investigations were more concerned with economic development than were Engels's somewhat crudely drawn parallels between classes in quite different economic circumstances. At various times Marx considered social changes that led, or *might* have led, to the introduction of

industrialised and bourgeois society into less developed conditions. Hence in the *Grundrisse* (written 1857–59) he looked into
pre-capitalist economic formations such as the late Roman
Empire (where industrial, bourgeois society could possibly
have developed, but did not). In other works Marx considered
the actual transition from feudal to bourgeois society in the
European context (in the Communist Manifesto, drawn from
Engels's 'Principles of Communism') and in particular the
formation of capitalism in Britain (in *Capital*). He was also
interested in the impact of bourgeois society on non-indus-
trialised communities, such as India and Russia, where he
attributed terrific strength to capitalist forces for modern-
isation, though he never ruled out entirely some alternative
mode of development – just as one would expect, given his
rejection of a philosophy of history and any historical 'master-
key' (SC 313).

The *Origin of the Family, Private Property and the State* was
an ambitious work by Engels, written between March and May
1884, using Marx's manuscripts from 1880–81. The work was
first published in 1884 and the final text established for the
fourth German edition in 1891. Marx had taken an interest in
Lewis Henry Morgan's *Ancient Society* (1877), in which the
author argued that technological progress in production
played the determining role for human development in a series
of stages from savagery through barbarism to civilisation. The
nature of production, what makes it peculiarly human, how
exactly it changed and developed, what social arrangements
arose as a result, what arrangements could have arisen instead,
and why social change took the course that it did – all were
problems set for himself by Marx. *The German Ideology*
represents his first attempt (with Engels's help) to get to grips
with the historical aspects of those inquiries and thus to shed
light on current patterns of change in society. *The German
Ideology* did not deal with pre-history, except briefly and
stipulatively, since factual material and anthropological speculation were not readily available. The so-called ethnological
notebooks left by Marx (and used by Engels) represent further
inquiries into human social development in pre-historical
times, once material of some repute in Morgan (and of
polemical interest in other authors) was available.

Engels abandoned much of Marx's scepticism about Morgan's work and turned his inquiries into 'conclusions', allegedly common to Marx and Morgan, supporting the truth of the 'materialist conception' in which 'the determining factor in history is, in the last resort, the production and reproduction of immediate life'. This was, of course, another re-write of Marx's 'guiding thread' of 1859, but incorporating the phrase 'in the last resort' and altering Marx's 'determines' to 'determining factor'. This way of presenting Marx's hypothesis as a 'law' reproduces the ambiguous materialism introduced in Engels's review of Marx's *A Contribution to the Critique of Political Economy*, which departs significantly from Marx with respect to analytical purpose, status of the matter – consciousness dichotomy, and theoretical scope.

In his introduction to what was basically his own work in *The Origin of the Family, Private Property and the State*, Engels linked Marx to the substantive views he was putting forward, and linked himself (with apparent, but imprecisely defined modesty) to Marx's 'investigations' (SW 449). He was by no means limited, however, to introducing his own works in this fashion. In the years between Marx's death and his own Engels composed no less than seventeen prefaces to works by Marx, and five to the jointly written Communist Manifesto; a total of twenty-two introductory essays, almost two a year. Before his death, Marx introduced the reader to his own published works, and Engels did likewise. During the 1880s and 1890s republication of Marx's works vastly increased, and there were in addition the second and third volumes of *Capital*, edited by Engels from Marx's manuscripts. The Marx–Engels intellectual relationship, as it has come down to us – a story of complete agreement expressed in interchangeable or supplementary works, the division of labour within a perfect partnership – was largely a creation of this period. It emerged from what Engels did, what he said, and what was implied in both.

The introductory summaries of Marx's work offered by Engels inclined at first towards the 'new' materialism of *The German Ideology* (and other works by Marx), and then later to the materialism of nature, history and 'thought' encompassed in Engels's dialectical laws. The ambiguity between the two materialisms remained (whichever side was emphasised), and Marx's writings reached subsequent readers with this puzzling prolegomenon.

The initial attempts by Engels to encapsulate the 'Marxist outlook' for the reader of posthumous editions of Marx's works were fairly close to his 'new' materialism. Engels's 1883 preface to a German edition of the Communist Manifesto seems a straightforward paraphrase of Marx's 1859 Preface to *A Contribution to the Critique of Political Economy*, though Engels has characteristically substituted 'political and intellectual history' for Marx's 'legal and political superstructure... and definite forms of social consciousness'. The effect, while apparently slight, is to give Marx's 'guiding thread' a somewhat academic character – tracing the linkage between past thoughts and events to recorded economic facts. Marx's formulation was more obviously general with respect to time, and therefore more obviously applicable to the analysis of the current events which mould the future. Moreover Marx's 'foundation' was merely that; on it *arose* political activities. Engels's 'foundation' was one *for* political and intellectual historiography, again implying that what was at issue were linkages that existed and needed only to be traced in order to demonstrate the truth (and utility, in some academic sense) of the materialist conception (SW 1.24; SW 181).

In his 1885 'On the History of the Communist League', written as an introduction to the third edition of Marx's *The Cologne Communist Trial*, Engels put Marx's view in much the same way. He connected it with the development of a new way of writing *history*, emphasising the academic slant to the interpretation of Marx's 1859 'guiding thread'. Engels's texts of 1883 and 1885 put the class struggle into an essentially academic context:

Preface (1883) to the Communist Manifesto	'On the History of the Communist League'
The basic thought running through the Manifesto – that economic production and the structure of society of every historical epoch necessarily arising there-	...speaking generally, it is not the state which conditions and regulates civil society, but civil society which conditions and regulates the state, and, conse-

from constitute the foundation for the political and intellectual history of that epoch; that consequently (ever since the dissolution of the primeval communal ownership of land) all history has been a history of class struggles, of struggles between exploited and exploiting, between dominated and dominating classes at various stages of social development; that this struggle, however, has now reached a stage where the exploited and oppressed class (the proletariat) can no longer emancipate itself from the class which exploits and oppresses it (the bourgeoisie), without at the same time forever freeing the whole of society from exploitation, oppression and class struggles – this basic thought belongs solely and exclusively to Marx (SW 1.24–5).

quently, that policy and its history are to be explained from the economic relations and their development, and not *vice versa*... This discovery, which revolutionised the science of history and, as we have seen, is essentially the work of Marx – a discovery in which I can claim for myself only a very insignificant share – was, however, of immediate importance for the contemporary workers' movement... These movements now presented themselves as a movement of the modern oppressed class, the proletariat, as the more or less developed forms of its historically necessary struggle against the ruling class, the bourgeoisie; as forms of the class struggle, but distinguished from all earlier class struggles by this one thing, that the present-day oppressed class, the proletariat, cannot achieve its emancipation without at the same time emancipating society as a whole from division into classes and, therefore, from class struggles (SW 2.344–5).

However, in his 'History of the Communist League' Engels produced an ambiguous qualification to his view that the new interpretation of history 'is essentially the work of Marx', when he wrote that (in effect) he had come to the same opinion independently in Manchester; he then referred to their 'joint work' as a 'detailed elaboration of the newly won mode of outlook in the most varied directions', curiously traducing Marx's focus, even in polemic, on the critique of political economy as the anatomy of *contemporary* civil society (SW 2.344). If we put this account together with the treatment of the period in Engels's *Ludwig Feuerbach and the End of Classical German Philosophy* (the two were written within a few months of each other), we can resolve some of the ambiguity by distinguishing between a common insight into the relation between activity and political life, and Marx's pithy critique of all previous materialism in the *Theses on Feuerbach*. Engels hailed the letter as the 'brilliant germ of the new world-outlook' incorporating its 'main features' (SW 585). That sort of work fascinated Engels, as he became more oriented towards philosophical issues; hence he promoted it to pride of place above *The German Ideology*, quite the opposite of Marx's comments in his 1859 Preface.

Then in his 1885 introduction to the third German edition of Marx's *Eighteenth Brumaire of Louis Bonaparte* (written by Marx between December 1851 and March 1852 as an analysis of French politics, 1848 to 1851), Engels appointed Marx 'historian' of the Second Republic and connected his work with what we know from Engels's other works of the 1880s to be 'dialectical' materialism:

It was precisely Marx who had first discovered the great law of motion of history, the law according to which all historical struggles, whether they proceed in the political, religious, philosophical or some other ideological domain, are in fact only the more or less clear expression of struggles of social classes, and that the existence and thereby the collisions, too, between these classes are in turn conditioned by the degree of development of their economic position, by the mode of their production and of their exchange determined by it. This law, which has the same significance for history as the law of the transformation of energy has for natural science – this law gave him here, too, the key to an understanding of the history of the Second French Republic (SW 1.246).

Similarly Engels's 1895 introduction to Marx's republished *Class Struggles in France 1848–50*, to which the *Eighteenth Brumaire* was a sequel, took Marx to be a historian, albeit of contemporary events, whose job was 'to trace political events back to effects of what were, in the final analysis, economic causes'. Engels's first difficulty was to explain how Marx could do this, given Engels's statement that 'a clear survey of the economic history of a given period can never be obtained

contemporaneously, but only subsequently, after a collecting
and sifting of the material has taken place'. Since all this
statistical material was patently unavailable to Marx at the
time of writing, he had, so Engels claimed, to modify his
methodology:

> For this reason, it is only too often necessary, in current history, to
> treat this, the most decisive, factor as constant, and the economic
> situation existing at the beginning of the period concerned as given
> and unalterable for the whole period, or else to take notice of only
> such changes in this situation as arise out of the patently manifest
> events themselves, and are, therefore, likewise patently manifest
> (SW 1.119).

Marx was actually doing something close to what Engels
described – 'tracing political conflicts back to the struggles
between the interests of the existing social classes and fractions
of classes created by the economic development', and proving
'the particular political parties to be the more or less adequate
political expression of these same classes and fractions of
classes'. Engels, however, viewed this as something to which
Marx as a 'materialist' *had to limit himself*, because it was at
odds with Engels's notion of 'a comprehensive presentation of
current history' and therefore in itself a source of error:

> It is self-evident that this unavoidable neglect of contemporaneous
> changes in the economic situation, the very basis of all the processes
> to be examined, must be a source of error. But all the conditions of a
> comprehensive presentation of current history unavoidably include
> sources of error – which, however, keeps nobody from writing
> current history (SW 1.119).

According to Engels, the subsequent consideration of 'the
economic history of the last ten years' had proved Marx's
conclusions in *The Class Struggles in France* and *The Eighteenth
Brumaire of Louis Bonaparte*, to be correct, as if there were little
warrant for believing in the soundness of Marx's work at the
time he wrote it. Marx's actual work in those two essays was
oriented more towards the future than the past, and its avowed
function was the explanation of revolutionary failure and the
explication of revolutionary prospects, both short- and long-

term. Marx's works were intended to have an interactive relationship with their audience and hence with revolutionary prospects as such; his function was not merely to deduce (somehow) past prospects and events from economic statistics as some kind of academic exercise in demonstrating 'causal' connections between phenomena already known. Hence Engels's apologies for Marx's political analysis are otiose, and his claim that Marx's 'inner connections' or 'law' brilliantly stood a 'double test' is grotesque compared with the actual results of Marx's investigations in the *Eighteenth Brumaire* (SW 1.119–21). In that work, almost in defiance of the 1859 generalisations which Engels took to be 'laws', the state was declared to be (in a sense) 'completely independent' of civil society; one political faction was defined as a clique of republican-minded individuals rather than the representative of a class-fraction arising from particular conditions of production; and a 'mediocrity' (Louis Bonaparte) was said to have risen *above* the class struggle to play a hero's part (SW 1.244, 257, 333). Marx's method was as much to discover discrepancies between current politics and his hypothesis as to document instances where they coincided. The discrepancies, in his view, represented potential instability, in which revolutionaries would be well advised to take an interest (see Carver (1982), chs 4–6).

Over the twelve years between Marx's death and his own on 5 August 1895, Engels established a series of ambiguities concerning what would otherwise have been fairly (though not completely) straightforward issues. After he promoted his own views in his works and prefaces of this period, the exact tenets of the 'new' materialism became obscure and the precise sense in which it was materialist was left unresolved. Whether that conception was the joint or independent invention of Marx and Engels or the sole invention of Marx could not be determined from what Engels had said, and what exactly the new conception was *for* became such an issue that Marx's works and methods were cut to fit Engels's account. Indeed the exact scope of Marx's work, Engels's work and their joint works became contentious, since after a time Engels began to drag Marx's works along in the wake of his own intellectual ambitions. As a result, the issue of authorship emerged – whether Engels spoke for himself alone, or whether he had Marx's specific or even general approval to speak for both.

The Marx–Engels intellectual relationship has interposed itself between us and the authors' respective works. This has happened because Engels presented himself as Marx's 'second fiddle', and because that is the way he is usually portrayed (MEW 36.218). In terms of his personal relationship to the living Marx, that image is largely accurate. The intellectual relationship between the two living men, however, was very much a story of what they accomplished independently, though their accomplishments were by no means theoretically coincident. As surviving partner, Engels moved into an all-powerful role as Marx's literary executor, political heir and apparently authoritative interpreter. He invented dialectics and reconstructed Marx's life and works accordingly. From our point of view, Engels's hindsight has come to obscure the Marx–Engels intellectual relationship, the story of what the two men actually said and did.

Conclusion

In the preceding chapter we saw how Engels's 'system' was substantively identified (by Engels) with Marx's 'outlook' and how Marx's own works were judged against the 'system', not always favourably. An examination of Engels's works, particularly his prefaces to *Anti-Dühring*, his best known work, revealed how his view of his relationship with Marx changed as the process of system-building progressed. The relationship was presented to his readers, in retrospect, as more collaborative on theoretical matters than it actually was. Moreover various assertions of a self-conscious division of labour between the two men were made and there were suggestions (from Engels) that their works were interchangeable, even up to the effective substitution of Engels's for Marx's. This has obscured important theoretical issues, because of the discrepancy between the different views put forward by Marx and by Engels as independent writers. This occurred particularly with respect to materialism and science, where Engels introduced crucial ambiguities (concerning matter in motion and scientific 'laws'); he also ascribed to Marx's works a quasi-Hegelian scope, an academic and retrospective character, a bogus dialectic and a factitious metaphysics. The effect of this process has been to neutralise contrary evidence, because Marx's works have been characteristically understood as coinciding wholly, largely, or partly, with Engels's reading of his social theory. Moreover Engels has been assumed to be the first authority on Marx's life and career, so what needs to be proved has been taken as true, without open-minded investigation.

The Marx–Engels relationship *matters*. Potentially a very great deal turns on how it is portrayed. Because millions adhere to Marxism, or are governed by those who do (or are perhaps constrained because they say they do), the tenets of Marxism are politically crucial throughout the world. Even when these are not domestically significant, the perception of foreign Marxism may play a role in determining decisions that have very wide-ranging effects.

The tenets of Marxism are open to negotiation, at least in some circles, and even where negotiation is prohibited, new ideas have a way of seeping in, albeit slowly. Obviously Marx's own works are the principal standard to which 'a Marxism', however well developed by subsequent thinkers, must adhere, or at least be related in some explicable way. If Marx has been amended, adapted or even rejected, an explanation must be found. The interpretation of his works is clearly the fundamental point on which any tenet of 'a Marxism' can be judged.

How his works are interpreted depends very much on what view of the Marx–Engels relationship is adopted. If Engels is co-equal, or even superior in certain respects – as he is if his works are taken in preference to Marx's or are taken as glosses so definitive that they come to stand for the original – then Marx's work will be understood in quite a different manner than it would if Engels's works were not given precedence. Because of Engels's personal role in setting himself, with all due modesty, beside Marx and because of the subsequent inflation of his views into Marxism as an official 'ideology', it has become a considerable exercise to read Marx without the benefit of an intervening layer of interpretation. Because of Engels's views, largely publicised and popularised after Marx's death, many comments by Marx have acquired new meaning and altered significance, indeed his whole critical attack on capitalist society was put in quite a different light. Thus we are unlikely to see what Marx said, and even less likely to see what he was doing, because 'what everyone knows to be true about Marx' is very largely a construct of the elderly Engels. That construct is difficult to dispose of, because by its very nature it tends to absorb the only material which could undermine it – a fresh reading of Marx's work that did not benefit from the hindsight that Engels cultivated in the 1880s and 1890s.

In particular Marx's project was implicitly redefined by Engels, interpretative categories were imposed on his work, and method was emphasised over content. Irrelevant questions were introduced and ambiguities were established in what was otherwise a complex but disciplined, even theoretically restrained body of work. Engels saw Marx as a historical scientist, establishing retrospectively the validity of his method and the truth of his 'laws' of society in general (not merely the accuracy of his laws of capitalist society detailed in his critique of political economy). In order to explain these 'laws' Engels introduced a standard mode of interpreting Marx's thought, according to which the neophyte must confront various philosophical issues through an explication of the concepts materialism and idealism, covering traditional points in ontology, epistemology and metaphysics. Engels promoted Hegel to a place above all other philosophers and made Marx his worthy successor, whose triumph was to rescue the dialectic – explicated in terms of contradictory and interactive relations – from idealism and to make it one with materialist premises (ambiguously defined).

The actual thrust of Marx's work, from 1842 onwards, was towards the revolutionary transformation of capitalist society; his critique of political economy was conceived as a contribution to that process, because in it he aimed to reveal the ineluctable logic of capitalist relations and the inevitable stresses that beset such a system, particularly with respect to the role of workers, whose interests, Marx argued, were ultimately opposed to those of other classes and to the further existence of class-divided society itself. While Marx's analysis is, in detail, by no means easy to follow, its very outlines are obscured by treating it, as Engels did, as a philosophical 'system' and 'world outlook' requiring a complex (and in his hands) mystifying prolegomenon. That this prolegomenon is founded on a revival of the very battles, indeed the very *kind* of battles, that Marx deplored as irrelevant to the political task at hand, is surely an appalling irony. Even if we stand back from the political context in which Marx's work becomes truly intelligible, and consider, in an academic way, what sort of ontology, epistemology (though never, I think, metaphysics) that Marx's work implies, there can be no valid claim that

Engels's work, taken as a whole, has added much to that discussion. This is because of his insensitivity to philosophical issues and his inability to define terms without generating ambiguities, deficiencies which prohibit his saying anything consistent. It is possible to find in Engels's work certain passages that do not apparently depart from Marx's premises and substantial contributions to social theory; other statements by Engels, however, inevitably obscure such points that might salvage his reputation as a commentator.

The contrast between Engels's earlier and later roles with respect to Marx and his work could hardly be more drastic. The younger Engels, before the real foundation of the partnership in late 1844 and early 1845, was in a sense a more influential and more accomplished, even more comprehensively independent writer than Marx. He was free-lance, international and politically gifted, as Marx was not. His breadth of subject-matter made him highly publishable, and his sheer analytical gifts – in political economy, in empirical social analysis, and even in social history (in broad outlines) – made him obviously attractive to the fiercely scrupulous Marx as a useful associate in promoting a communist movement that was genuinely in touch, in theory and practice, with the potentially revolutionary classes in society. Whether Marx was crucially dependent on the insights of the early Engels, particularly on the role of industrial production in modern society and of production in human life in general, cannot really be determined. Similarly it cannot be shown that Marx required an Engels to bring the historical and empirical circumstances of English industrialisation to his attention. But, as I have argued, Engels certainly provided Marx with a considerable short-cut in getting from his intellectually penetrating, yet politically, geographically and stylistically circumscribed journalism to the (comparative) vocational clarity of the *Economic and Philosophical Manuscripts* of 1844, the theoretical self-clarification recorded in *The German Ideology*, and the political clarion-call of the Communist Manifesto.

However, the theoretical, empirical and even in some respects political and historical virtues of Engels's work were substantially degraded when he settled into his role as Marx's 'second fiddle', introducing and popularising his works.

Though these accounts bore Engels's name (or were written by him and published anonymously), they were in a sense less his own than the earlier works written before the partnership was established. The later works always bore some implicit or, more usually, explicit relationship to those of Marx; the earlier works, which I have praised, perhaps overmuch, at least had qualities of freshness and directness surmounting the limits of discipleship that makes them appealing and persuasive. In them there is a sense of Engels giving his own account of the subject under consideration; in later works we find a ponderous, pompous quality in which Engels assures us of Marx's achievements, which he then proceeds to amplify in an oddly de-personalised yet Olympian way. Such enthusiasm as comes through in the later works is manifested in an unrestrained philosophising quite foreign to Marx's thought, unedifying in itself and covertly self-congratulatory in a way that never appeared in the early, pre-partnership writings.

Although Engels's early works were really his own, in a sense not duplicated in the later, more derivative reviews and introductions, they were rather too various, lacking a coherent focus and sense of vocation. But Marx's work on political economy, even when pursued in a polemical context, and even when polemic itself seemed to overshadow this unifying vocation, had just this quality to give it coherence. Engels found his vocation in 1859, rather unfortunately, as systematising philosopher, setting Marx's work in an academic and philosophical context, drawing out its implications as a universal methodology, and adding what was declared in advance to be consistent with it, a positivist account of natural science. Engels had a tendency to push Marx's work back into the traditional academic moulds of philosophy, history and economics. Having had little formal higher education, he lacked the scepticism so thoroughly displayed by Marx towards the way that professional academics divide up human experience.

Engels's commentaries on Marx display a double aspect: class analysis and philosophical materialism. They present a class analysis which squares with works such as *The German Ideology*, the Communist Manifesto and *The Eighteenth Brumaire of Louis Bonaparte*, though Engels's analysis tended towards an unsubtle linkage between politics and technology.

Marx had a deeper perspective which reached from the broad sweep of capitalist development down to the sometimes quite contrary activities of politicians.

The more serious discrepancy between the two, however, was Engels's move, sometime in the 1850s, from Marx's view of science as an *activity* important in technology and industry, to seeing its importance for socialists in terms of a *system* of knowledge, incorporating the causal laws of physical science and taking them as a model for a covertly academic study of history, 'thought' and, somewhat implausibly, current politics. While we have no direct evidence on when or how this shift in Engels's work occurred, it seems reasonable to attribute it to his interest in technological innovation (important in his family business and of obvious interest to his Manchester associates) and to his contacts with physical scientists themselves, some of whom became his friends. After abandoning, as it were, his previous work on political economy and empirical social studies to Marx, Engels filled the gap with an expansion of his historical and political efforts within a quasi-Hegelian framework which, like, many frameworks, dominated the attention of the social scientist.

What his later works lost in authorial authenticity, Engels made up through his vocation as Marxist theoretician, foremost authority on a comprehensive, and comprehensively valid *Weltanschauung*. Anything further from Marx's investigative, rigorous and independent approach to the politics of capitalist society is difficult to imagine. While the drift in Engels's career is now apparent to us, because of our knowledge of his manuscripts and of works written after 1883, this material was largely unknown (and most of it was *certainly* unknown) to Marx. Hence the view that he consented tacitly to Engels's system-building and to its tenets cannot be sustained. It is almost as if the Marx–Engels relationship occurred twice, once in Marx's lifetime, for which we read the historical record forwards, and once again during the years in which Engels survived him. For Engels's view of the relationship the historical record is read backwards, taking his conclusions as given and glossing texts and facts to fit these pre-ordained truths. While interesting as an intellectual artifact, and overwhelmingly influential as an approach to Marx's life-work, the second-hand, retrospective view derived from Engels has all the defects of anachronism, hindsight and specious argument from authority. These are defects I hope I have avoided in examining the intellectual relationship of Karl Marx and Friedrich Engels.

Marx–Engels Chronology

	Marx		Engels
5 May 1818	Born at Trier		
		29 Nov. 1820	Born at Barmen
Sept. 1835	Leaves school		
Oct. 1835	Enters Bonn University		
Oct. 1836	Enters Berlin University		
		Sept. 1837	Leaves school; enters family firm
		Autumn 1838	Moves to Bremen; publishes poems
Jan. 1839	Begins Doctoral Dissertation		
		Spring 1839	Publishes 'Letters from Wuppertal'; associates with Young Germany
		Summer 1840	Visits England; reads Hegel
		Spring 1841	Leaves Bremen for Barmen
April 1841	Submits Doctoral Dissertation to University of Jena		
		Sept. 1841	Leaves Barmen for Berlin
		Early 1842	Publishes attacks on Schelling; associates with

Date	Marx	Date	Engels
		April 1842	Young Hegelians; joins 'The Free' First published contribution to *Rheinische Zeitung*
May 1842	Publishes in *Rheinische Zeitung* on press freedom		
		Mid-1842	Publishes in *Rheinische Zeitung* on press freedom and on other liberal issues
Oct. 1842	Edits *Rheinische Zeitung*; publishes on 'Theft of Wood'	Oct. 1842	Meets Moses Hess in Cologne
Nov. 1842	Attacks 'The Free'; first meets Engels, receiving him 'coldly'	Nov. 1842	First meets Marx; leaves Germany for England
		Late 1842	Publishes on English politics and socialism
		Early to mid-1843	Publishes on communism
Jan. 1843	Publishes on poor in Mosel valley		
March 1843	*Rheinische Zeitung* disbanded; begins 'Letters'		
Mid-1843	Writes *Critique of Hegel's Philosophy of Right*		
Oct. 1843	Moves from Germany to Paris		
		Late 1843	Writes 'Outlines of a Critique of Political Economy'
Nov. 1843	Receives Engels's 'Outlines'		
Early 1844	Summarises Engels's 'Outlines';	Early 1844	*Deutsch-Französische*

	Marx		Engels
	Deutsch-Französische Jahrbücher published; Marx contributes 'Letters', *On the Jewish Question* and 'Critique of Hegel's Philosophy of Right. Introduction'		*Jahrbücher* published; Engels contributes 'Outlines' and review of Carlyle; begins research on *Condition of the Working Class in England*
April 1844	Begins *Economic and Philosophical Manuscripts*		
End Aug. 1844	Meets Engels again; founds partnership; begins *The Holy Family* with Engels	End Aug. 1844	Agrees to collaborate with Marx; begins *The Holy Family*
		Sept. 1844	Leaves Paris for Barmen
Autumn 1844	Begins correspondence with Engels	Autumn 1844	Publishes 'Condition of England' articles
Nov. 1844	Completes *The Holy Family*		
Jan. 1845	Expelled from France		
Feb. 1845	Arrives in Brussels	Feb. 1845	Gives speeches in Elberfeld
Spring 1845	Signs contract for *Critique of Politics and Political Economy*; writes *Theses on Feuerbach*	Spring 1845	Joins Marx in Brussels
Mid-1845	Visits Manchester with Engels	Mid-1845	Takes Marx to Manchester
Sept. 1845	Begins *The German Ideology* with Engels		
		Autumn 1845 to summer 1846	Works with Marx

			on *The German Ideology*
1846–7	Works with Brussels Correspondence Committee	1846–7	Works with Brussels Correspondence Committee
Early 1847	Joins Communist League	Early 1847	Writes on 'True Socialists'; joins Communist League; drafts 'Communist Confession of Faith' and (later) 'Principles of Communism'
Dec. 1847	Works on Communist Manifesto	Dec. 1847	Works on Communist Manifesto
Jan. 1848	Finishes Communist Manifesto		
Aug. 1849	Moves to London		
		Late 1849	Joins Marx in London
1850	Publishes *The Class Struggles in France*	1850	Publishes *The Peasant War in Germany*
		Nov. 1850	Moves to Manchester
Late 1851 to early 1852	Writes and then publishes *The Eighteenth Brumaire of Louis Bonaparte*	Late 1851 to early 1852	Writes and then publishes *Revolution and Counter-Revolution in Gemany* (signed Marx)
1857–9	Writes *Grundrisse* manuscripts		
1859	Publishes *A Contribution to the Critique of Political Economy* (with Preface)		
		Aug. 1859	Reviews Marx's *Contribution*

1867	Publishes volume one of *Capital*		
		1868	Reviews Marx's *Capital*
		1869	Publishes short biography of Marx; retires from business
1872	Publication date of 2nd edn of *Capital*		
Jan. 1873	Date of Afterword to 2nd edn of *Capital*		
		Early 1873	Starts *Dialectics of Nature*
		May 1876	Decides to write *Anti-Dühring*
1877	Contributes 'Dühringiana' on political economy		
Nov. 1877	Writes to 'Editorial Board' on 'philosophy of history'		
		1877–8	Publishes *Anti-Dühring* as articles, pamphlet and book
1880	Publishes Preface (signed Paul Lafargue) to Engels's *Socialism, Utopian and Scientific*	1880	Publishes *Socialism, Utopian and Scientific*
1880–1	Writes Ethnological Notebooks		
14 March 1883	Dies in London		
		Mid-1883	Publishes Preface to new edition of Communist Manifesto
		1884	Publishes *Origin of the Family,*

	Private Property and the State
1885	Date of Preface to 2nd edn of *Anti-Dühring*; publishes introduction to 3rd edn of Marx's *Eighteenth Brumaire*; publishes 'On the History of the Communist League'
1886	Publishes 2nd edn of *Anti-Dühring*; publishes *Ludwig Feuerbach and the End of Classical German Philosophy* as review
1888	Publishes *Ludwig Feuerbach* as a book
1891	Publishes 4th edn of *Origin of the Family, Private Property and the State*
1892	Publishes English edn of *Socialism, Utopian and Scientific* (with Preface)
1894	Publishes 3rd edn of *Anti-Dühring* (with Preface)
1895	Publishes introduction to Marx's *Class Struggles in France*
5 Aug. 1895	Dies in London

Abbreviations and Bibliography

AD	Frederick Engels, *Anti-Dühring*, Lawrence & Wishart, London, 1947, repr. 1969.
CAP 1	Karl Marx, *Capital*, vol. 1, trans. Samuel Moore and Edward Aveling, ed. Frederick Engels, Lawrence & Wishart, London, 1954, repr. 1977.
Carver (1975)	Karl Marx, *Texts on Method*, trans. and ed. Terrell Carver, Blackwell, Oxford, 1975.
Carver (1976)	Terrell Carver, 'Marx – and Hegel's *Logic*', *Political Studies*, 24 (1976), 57–68.
Carver (1981)	Terrell Carver, *Engels* ('Past Masters'), Oxford University Press, Oxford, 1981.
Carver (1982)	Terrell Carver, *Marx's Social Theory* ('OPUS'), Oxford University Press, Oxford, 1982.
CCPE	Karl Marx, *A Contribution to the Critique of Political Economy*, trans. S.W. Ryazanskaya, ed. Maurice Dobb, Lawrence & Wishart, London, 1971.
CW	Karl Marx and Frederick Engels, *Collected Works*, Lawrence & Wishart, London, 1975 etc. [in progress]
DN	Frederick Engels, *Dialectics of Nature*, Foreign Languages Publishing House, Moscow, 1954.
Hegel (1837/1956)	G.W.F. Hegel, *Philosophy of History*, trans. J. Sibree, Dover, New York, 1956.
McLellan (1973)	David McLellan, *Karl Marx: His Life and Thought*, Macmillan, London, 1973.

MEGA (New Series) Karl   Marx   and   Friedrich   Engels,
                   Gesamtausgabe (MEGA), Dietz, Berlin, 1972
                   etc. [in progress]
MEGA (Old Series) Karl Marx and Friedrich Engels, *Historisch-
                   kritische Gesamtausgabe*, edd. D. Ryazanov
                   et al., Frankfurt and Berlin, 1927 etc.
                   [incomplete]
MEW   Karl Marx and Friedrich Engels, *Werke*,
                   Dietz, Berlin, 1956 etc. [completed]
SC   Karl Marx and Frederick Engels, *Selected
                   Correspondence*, trans. I. Lasker, 2nd edn,
                   Progress, Moscow, 1965.
SW   Karl Marx and Frederick Engels, *Selected
                   Works* in one volume, Lawrence & Wishart,
                   London, 1968, repr. 1973.
SW 1 or 2   Karl Marx and Frederick Engels, *Selected
                   Works* in two volumes, Lawrence & Wishart,
                   London, 5th imp., 1962.

I would like to assure the reader that I have used so many different
editions of the works of Marx and Engels purely out of necessity, not
choice.

OTHER WORKS CONSULTED:

Terence Ball, 'Marx and Darwin: A Reconsideration', *Political
Theory* 7 (1979), 469–84; for information on the latest research
concerning the Marx–Darwin relationship. A correspondence fol-
lows in subsequent numbers.
Norman Levine, *The Tragic Deception: Marx contra Engels*, Clio
Books, Oxford and Santa Barbara, 1975; the only other full-length
study.
W.O. Henderson, *The Life of Friedrich Engels*, 2 vols, Frank Cass,
London, 1976; invaluable as a factual source.
Sheldon S. Wolin, 'Political Theory as a Vocation', *American
Political Science Review* 63 (1969), 1062–82; particularly the de-
scription of 'methodism' on 1066-7.

Acknowledgements

For permission to use my previously published material I am grateful to Oxford University Press (*Engels*), to Cambridge University Press ('Marxism as Method' in *After Marx*, edd. Terence Ball and James Farr), and to *The Times Higher Educational Supplement* ('The Marx–Engels intellectual relationship'). Quotations from English editions of the works of Marx and Engels are published by permission of Lawrence & Wishart Ltd.

My thanks to Larry Wilde for reading the typescript and offering some stimulating counter-arguments.

Index